THE REAL HISTORY BEHIND
FOYLE'S
WAR

THE REAL HISTORY BEHIND
FOYLE'S
WAR

Foreword by **Anthony Horowitz**

ROD GREEN

CARLTON
BOOKS

THIS IS A CARLTON BOOK

First published in the UK by Carlton Books Ltd 2006
20 Mortimer Street
London W1T 3JW

Foyle's War ™ and ® Greenlit Rights Ltd 2006
Text and Design Copyright © Carlton Books Ltd 2006

Foyle's War is a Greenlit Rights production for ITV1

10-digit ISBN 1-84442-148-1
13-digit ISBN: 978-184442-148-0

Editorial Manager: Lorna Russell
Picture Research: Paul Langan
Design: Vicky Holmes & Anna Pow
Production: Lisa French

Printed in Dubai

CONTENTS

FOREWORD

From the very beginning, I never really thought of *Foyle's War* as a 'murder-mystery show'. I was always much more interested in exploring that unique period in our history: the Home Front from 1940 to the end of the war. And it seems to me that as the show has progressed, the murders with their clues, red herrings, the array of suspects and the (hopefully) surprise revelations at the end have almost taken a back seat.

But look at the ground we've covered! Anti-semitism, conscientious objectors, funk holes, the development of biological weapons, illegal gambling, homosexuality in the armed forces, the creation of the SOE, the first developments in plastic surgery, saboteurs, the arrival of the Americans, convoys, land girls, munitions workers, the bouncing bomb and so on – and on and on.

By the end of the sixth series, we will have made 19 two-hour episodes, and I will have written sixteen of them. I have drawn on well over a hundred books, but feel I should publicly acknowledge my two 'bibles': *The People's War* by Angus Calder and *How We Lived Then* by Norman Longmate. I also have to thank Terry Charman at the Imperial War Museum, a bottomless font of knowledge.

It seemed to me to be very important to get the details right. Not just out of respect for those who died, but because any distortion of history, even for dramatic purposes, is, I believe, a small crime – especially when the history is so recent and impacts so much on how we are now.

Last year, I had a letter from an American marine who was actually present on the convoy when the destroyer, the *Reuben James*, was sunk in 1941 with the loss of 115 lives. I had described that incident in Series Four, an episode called 'Invasion', and his letter, telling me what he saw that night, was another reminder that the Second World War is not quite history. Not yet. It is still living with us now.

So I'm particularly glad that this book has been written. We found so many remarkable untold stories when we were making the programme and here they all are – set down accurately and without the gloss of TV drama.

It has been a privilege working on *Foyle's War*. I hope it has done justice to an extraordinary time.

Anthony Horowitz

INTRODUCTION

Foyle's War has been widely praised for its engaging storylines, the admirable performances from the cast and the painstaking attention to detail in both its writing and filming that gives the series such an air of authority and authenticity. Every scene, every shot, is carefully considered to ensure that the realism achieved through the professionalism of the writers, the production crew and the cast is meticulously maintained. It is no accident, therefore, that Hastings was chosen as the location for the series. The old part of the town with its quaint buildings and winding streets is a conservation area where modern buildings do not intrude, making life a little easier for the film makers, although there are still many pitfalls to be avoided; modern road markings, signposts, television aerials and other elements inherent to today's urban townscapes must be concealed, disguised or excluded from the images that will ultimately appear on our TV screens.

But is Hastings, which many would surely assume to have been a sleepy seaside retreat during World War II, really a suitable setting for a drama that revolves around serious crime? Are DCS Christopher Foyle and his cohorts, Sergeant Paul Milner and driver Samantha Stewart, anything like the real police teams at work on the south coast of England during the war? Do the cases they investigate bear any relation to the sort of crimes perpetrated at that time? *Foyle's War: The Truth Behind The Fiction* provides an intriguing insight into law and order on the home front between 1939 and 1945, and reveals how true to real life the series actually is.

Far from being a sleepy backwater during the war, Hastings and St Leonards, along with much of the south coast of England, found itself in the front line. While Hastings was not subjected to the horror of the bombing 'blitzes' experienced by London, Coventry, Liverpool, Birmingham and other major population and industrial centres, including Portsmouth and Southampton on the south coast, it was nonetheless targeted many times. There were 85 enemy air raids on the town. The Luftwaffe dropped over 750 incendiaries as well as 550 high explosive bombs, and 15 V1 flying bombs fell on the area. More than 700 people were injured and 154 killed. The death of Sam's friend when their lodgings are bombed in the episode 'Fifty Ships' or the destruction of local pub and the death of a barmaid in 'The German Woman', sadly reflect actual events. In Hasting almost 450 houses were demolished either by direct hits or because bomb damage had left them too dangerously unstable to be allowed to remain standing. Almost half of the inhabitants were evacuated from the town, the pre-war population figure of 65,000 dropping to just 34,000 during hostilities. The evacuations were not only to keep people safe from the bombing but were deemed necessary because Hastings was expected to become one of the focal points of the imminent German invasion.

There was a great deal of military activity in the area. Seaside holidaymakers were banned, beach defences were established and road blocks set up. Military manoeuvres and invasion exercises such as the one featured in the 'War Games' episode were taken very seriously, training the Home Guard and

ABOVE: *Much of the old part of Hastings, where* Foyle's War *is set, has remained largely unchanged since the 1940s, the district having been made a conservation area.*

regular troops for the onslaught everyone believed was about to happen. As the Battle of Britain raged overhead, the fear that German troops were about to storm the beaches, a concern often expressed in the early episodes of *Foyle's War*, was very real indeed. German documents from the period show Hastings as part of the landing grounds to be taken by Assault Group 16 which was to embark at Calais for the trip across the English Channel. Despite the evacuations and the lack of seasonal visitors, during the war Hastings was busier than ever – and the criminal fraternity was among the busiest of all. It is little wonder that his superiors continually blocked Foyle's repeated requests for transfer to duties he felt would be more beneficial to the war effort. Experienced and reliable police officers were needed everywhere, not least in an area as sensitive as the south coast. Across the country the crime rate soared by 57 per cent during the war years. Murders increased by 22 per cent. Racketeers, black marketeers and gangsters involved in organised crime found

new opportunities opening up almost every day. The notorious gangster Mad Frankie Fraser was active during the war, describing the period as 'the best years of my life… Paradise… I'll never forgive Hitler for losing the war!' Fraser was involved in, amongst other enterprises, a raid on a warehouse where hundreds of bottles of whisky were stored ('You could get two quid a bottle for it') and the theft of ration coupons from a government depot.

The episode 'The Funk Hole' shows a raid by black marketeers on a Ministry of Food depot during which one of the thieves is shot by a member of the Home Guard. The ultimate penalty for stealing food in this way, or for looting, was death by hanging, although no one was actually hanged during the war for such an offence. Looting from bombed-out buildings was, however, a major problem. In the first two months of The Blitz in London almost 400 cases of looting were reported to the police, and of the first twenty looting trials at the Old Bailey, ten involved

BELOW: *Soldiers stand guard over the wreckage of a Messerschmitt Bf110 which crashed in the Sussex countryside near Hastings.*

members of the Auxiliary Fire Service, just as was portrayed in 'Fifty Ships'. Chief Inspector Percy Datlen of Dover CID, who would have been a contemporary of Foyle, reported that after one raid on the city, organised looting had been rife: 'In cases where there are several houses bombed out in one street, the looters have systematically gone through the lot. Carpets have been stripped from the floors, stair carpets have been removed: they have even taken away heavy mangles, bedsteads and complete suites of furniture. We believe it is the greatest organised looting that has yet taken place and many front line citizens who have returned to their homes to carry on their essential jobs are facing severe financial difficulties as a result of the work of the gang.'

Looting on such a large scale was the work of organised gangs, but many of the looters were little more than boys, teenagers too young to be called up for military service. These teenage 'blackout gangs' were so active that by early 1941 every remand centre in the country was full. The teenagers were just as much a danger to their victims and the police as were more experienced, hardened criminals; Home Guard armaments stores were regularly broken into and three 17-year-olds who stole loaded Sten sub-machine guns from a Home Guard store used them to hold up the Ambassador Cinema in Hayes. They later admitted to 43 other armed robberies. Police officers like Foyle and Milner remained unarmed during the course of their normal duties but firearms were so readily available to their criminal adversaries that they could easily find themselves being shot at, as happened to Foyle and Sam in Among The Few when the driver of a truckload of stolen fuel took pot shots at them.

The crimes featured in *Foyle's War* are as authentic as the uniforms, the vehicles or Andrew Foyle's Spitfire, but what of the characters themselves? Clearly a direct line can be drawn between Christopher Foyle and real-life police officers such as the aforementioned Chief Inspector Datlen. Sergeant Milner, too, invalided out of the

military, would have been welcomed back into the police service, although the loss of a leg might well have been deemed such a serious disability that he would have been confined to desk duties. Sam, on the other hand, is something of an anomaly. As a member of the MTC (Mechanised Transport Corps) Sam would have been a volunteer. Women were not conscripted for war work, or industrial service, until December 1941, but many volunteered prior to that, like the Land Army girls in 'They Fought In The Fields', in order to 'do their bit' for the war effort. Sam's work in the MTC would have involved her training as a mechanic and driver, but her driving duties would have been confined to military trucks or staff cars. It would have been most unusual for a member of the MTC to be seconded to the police service as the Women's Auxiliary Police Corps provided clerks, typists, telephonists and drivers for the police. Had there been no Auxiliary Police Corps driver available in Hastings, however, it is feasible that an MTC volunteer such as Sam might have been drafted in to work with Foyle.

Foyle's caseload would certainly have kept him busy. In 1939 the police in England and Wales dealt with a little over 300,000 arrestable offences, but as the war progressed that figure would more than double. While the commonly-held perception of our nation at war is that of the people standing shoulder-to-shoulder in the face of adversity, the activities of those who lurked in shadows of the blackout touched the lives of almost everyone. The housewife who managed to buy a cut of meat from the butcher that was in excess of her ration allowance was helping to encourage the profiteering of not only the butcher but also his suppliers and the farmers who kept undeclared livestock, just as the farmer in 'They Fought In The Fields' had done. Thefts from railway yards, dockyards and military depots were also rife, with everything from

cigarettes and chocolate to petrol and batteries disappearing onto the black market. The theft of fuel was central to the plot of 'Among The Few' while Foyle, depressed that he was not doing more for the war effort, actually complained of having to arrest a man for selling stolen batteries in 'The French Drop'.

A police officer of Foyle's seniority would, however, have been involved in many far more serious crimes than the peddling of stolen batteries. The beaches on the south coast, although strung with barbed wire and heavily guarded, were still tempting landing areas for German spies sent to Britain to report back on the effect of the Luftwaffe bombing campaign on civilian morale, troop movements, the locations of military installations and a host of other detailed information. Fortunately, the real German spies were generally as ill-prepared as the one captured in 'Fifty Ships'. His mistake in asking, in heavily accented English, for a beer at a pub at ten in the morning led directly to his arrest. Real spies made the same sort of error, blundering into military patrols near the coast while wearing wet clothing, asking for directions in an accent that aroused suspicion or, in the case of Carl Meier, walking into a pub in Lydd one morning after landing at Dungeness (not far from Hastings) and asking the landlady for a pint of cider outside of normal licensing hours. Of the 115 German spies who infiltrated Britain during the war every single one was identified by the security services, usually within hours of their arrival, and either 'turned' (used to supply misinformation to their spymasters) or, as was the case with Meier and his partner José Rudolf Waldberg, sent to the gallows.

Foyle's War: The Truth Behind The Fiction provides a review of the episodes from all four series as well as a wealth of background information on the living and working conditions for ordinary people during the war, the role of the police in wartime and the crimes on which the plotlines of *Foyle's War* are based.

1. THE ROLE OF THE POLICE IN WARTIME

There is a palpable feeling of anxiety in the early episodes of *Foyle's War* when, at the end of May 1940, Operation Dynamo brought every serviceable craft along the south coast of England into the war to evacuate Allied troops stranded at Dunkirk in France. In all, over 860 vessels were involved in plucking more than 330,000 servicemen from the beaches as the Germans laid siege to Dunkirk. The operation was seen as a triumph, but the British Army was left in disarray, struggling to re-equip in time to face what many expected to be the inevitable German invasion of southern England.

For police officers like Christopher Foyle the situation was even more distressing than for members of the general public. Foyle would have been more aware than most of the defences being constructed and the strategies that the military proposed to follow in the event of an invasion. The police had to work closely with the Home Guard and regular military authorities when, for example, roads were closed for military manoeuvres. Foyle, in fact, was required to participate in the Home Guard manoeuvres in the 'War Games' episode. Senior police officers knew, therefore, that the military authorities fully expected an invasion to happen. What they would not have known was just how far the Germans' preparations had progressed.

In July 1940 German units were issued with orders covering the invasion with different assault groups allocated landing areas stretching from Margate in the east all the way round to Weymouth. Around 2,000 invasion barges were assembled at various points along the French, Belgian and Dutch coasts with 90,000 troops prepared to storm the beaches between Folkestone and Brighton (Hastings is around halfway between the two). Hitler originally scheduled the invasion, codenamed Operation Sea Lion, for 15 September 1940, although the plan was later postponed to some time between 19 and 26 September.

The Germans knew they needed to have total air superiority in order to stage successful landings. If the RAF was able to operate in strength, their invasion fleet would be bombed into oblivion before it got near the landing grounds. The most dangerous elements of the Royal Navy's Home Fleet were stationed at Scapa Flow in Orkney, out of range of German bombers. It would take them two days to reach the English Channel to intervene in Operation Sea Lion, so the RAF posed the immediate threat. Hermann Göring, the Luftwaffe Commander-in-Chief, boasted that he would destroy the RAF in just four days with a massive air offensive against the airfields and radar stations as well as overwhelming numbers of fighter aircraft to shoot the British pilots out of the sky. The beginning of his campaign, dubbed *Aldertag* or 'Eagle Day' (taken as the title for Episode 4 of *Foyle's War*), was scheduled for 10 August but postponed due to bad weather. What became known as the Battle of Britain actually began around 12 August and raged not for the predicted four days, but for more than four weeks, culminating on 15 September when the RAF scrambled every

one of its fighters to combat the Luftwaffe's air armada. They destroyed 56 German aircraft that day, finally forcing Göring to admit that he could never dominate the skies over the south coast of England to provide the kind of protective umbrella that the invasion force would need. On 17 September, Hitler announced the indefinite postponement of Operation Sea Lion.

But what if things had worked out differently? What if Göring had succeeded in

crushing the RAF? The September invasion would have met stiff opposition, but what would it have meant for the ordinary people on the south coast of England? What would it have meant for Foyle and his team?

Hastings, like seaside towns all around the coast of Britain, was heavily fortified at the outbreak of war. The town's beaches were festooned with barbed wire, gun emplacements, steel and concrete obstructions to stop tanks landing, minefields and even pipe-work through which it was intended to pump fuel to form a flame defence system. On 14 October 1940, the anniversary of the Battle of Hastings, the defences were further augmented by a battery of anti-aircraft guns which were ultimately to line the foreshore along Sea Road.

The pier, like the one at neighbouring St Leonard's and countless others around the country, was sectioned, part of it being removed so that the main pier structure was

LEFT: *The distinctive black-painted multi-storey beach huts on the seafront at Hastings are used by fishermen to dry their nets. The huts featured in 'The German Woman', the very first episode of Foyle's War.*

no longer connected to the shore. Ironically, British seaside resorts had developed piers in the nineteenth century before there were efficient road or rail networks to allow larger steam ships that could not approach the beach, or for which the local harbour was too shallow, to bring holidaymakers into the resorts. They would disembark from the ships onto the piers. Later, piers became an extension of the promenade and were used primarily for leisure rather than as landing stages, but in World War II there was an obvious danger that invading Germans might attempt to use the piers for their original purpose. Hastings' pier was, therefore, cut in half. The loss of the pleasure pier would have made little difference to anyone out to enjoy the resort's facilities as the beaches were strictly out of bounds to the general public. Hastings' fishermen were allowed onto the beach from which they launched their boats, although their work at sea became ever more dangerous, with several boats lost to mines.

The military authorities had prepared Hastings to become a battleground, but had the Germans stormed the beaches it is unlikely that they would have been repulsed. In 1974, at Sandhurst, the Royal Military Academy, staff officers and military historians used all of the information that had by then become available to examine both the German invasion plans and the British defences.

Compared to the years of planning that went into the Allies' D-Day operation in 1944, the Germans' 1940 invasion plans appear somewhat inadequate. The Allies had the experience of the disastrous Dieppe raid in August 1942 and the lessons learned in amphibious combined operations through the landing of troops in North Africa during Operation Torch in November 1942, the invasion of Sicily in July 1943 and the landings on the Italian mainland in September 1943. The Germans, on the other

ABOVE: *The Mayor of Hastings inspects an anti-aircraft gun in August 1944. A battery of such guns was installed along the esplanade on Sea Road on 14 October 1940, the anniversary of the Battle of Hastings.*

ABOVE: *Much of the south coast of England offered tempting landing grounds for a German invasion and Hastings was designated an area of special importance, or 'nodal point' in the British Army's defence plans. Here Captain Halliday (Philip Franks) looks out over the Channel in 'Bad Blood'.*

hand, had never attempted amphibious operations on such a scale. They had mounted successful river crossings under fire, but nothing like the kind of operation that would be required to storm the beaches along the south coast of England.

Nevertheless, the Germans assembled their fleet of invasion barges. The majority of these were extremely shallow-draught vessels requisitioned from inland waterways and fitted with ramps at the bows that would drop down when the craft hit the beaches. Most of these barges, however, had no means of propulsion. On the European canals they were generally towed by tugs. They would also have to be towed or pushed across the English Channel by tugs or minesweepers. Designed for use on calm, sheltered waterways, the barges would have fared rather badly in the choppy, open water of the Channel. Troop training exercises were conducted, however, in embarkation at French ports and in beach landings, some of the landing operations taking place on the French shoreline at Calais, within sight of the English coast. Remarkably, the hundreds of tugs, motor-boats and passenger ferries earmarked for the invasion were required to transport not only men and equipment but also the thousands of horses that the German army relied upon to pull field guns and supply wagons.

While their preparations for the invasion may appear ill-conceived, the strategists at Sandhurst believed that, had the RAF been subdued and the invasion gone ahead, the Germans would have taken the beaches. With a force of around 8,000 paratroops dropped to secure their exits from the landing areas, within 48 hours the invaders could have pushed up to eight miles inland. Then, said the Sandhurst experts, they would have started to run into problems.

The headlong rush across country during their 'blitzkrieg' campaigns in Europe would have been thwarted in the English countryside. Throughout the summer of 1940, hundreds of thousands of workers laboured in fields and by the roadsides all across Britain constructing a maze of military defences. In the south of England, every bridge and crossroads was defended by its own pillbox gun emplacement, or concrete road block with booby traps. Not one of them would have held up the German advance for long. Each was designed to buy a little time, together hindering the enemy long enough to allow British forces, along with the Canadians and the remnants of the Polish and French armies, to rally around the major defensive positions, or 'stop lines', that had been constructed. If you travel through the countryside in Britain today, you can see the occasional World War II concrete pillbox still standing, seemingly alone and exposed in a field. In fact, the pillbox would have been surrounded by its own network of trenches and machine-gun nests, and would almost certainly have been in line of sight with the next pillbox in a chain that could stretch for miles. These stop lines criss-crossed the country at strategic points, and it was at the first major stop line from the coast that Sandhurst's strategists believed the German advance would have ground to a halt.

The Winston Line was about 15 miles inland from the beaches and the Germans were expected to have reached there by the third day. Britain's mobile reserve would have been waiting in readiness to engage them and the German troops, weary after the long, hard-fought slog up from the beaches, would probably not have been ideally prepared for this major confrontation. By now their supplies would be running low as Royal Navy reinforcements from Scapa Flow in Orkney arrived in the English Channel, breaking

through the minefields sown by the Germans to protect their invasion fleet. The ships essential to the resupply of the German invasion would have been sunk. Starved of supplies, the German army on English soil would have quickly run out of food and ammunition. Driven back to the beaches with no ships to evacuate them and no Dunkirk fleet of little boats to rescue them, many thousands would have been captured.

The most optimistic prognosis from the Sandhurst strategists was that the Germans might have lasted about a week on British soil. They also believed that the fighting would have wreaked havoc in the countryside of Kent and Sussex, devastating many of the villages caught up in the conflict. Those of the British civilian population who had not been evacuated from the area would have had to endure a terrifying experience and there would have been a great many civilian casualties. It was in protecting and controlling the civilian population that Foyle and police officers like him would have faced their greatest challenge.

Any policeman of Foyle's seniority, and with his World War I military experience, would have appreciated the horrors that awaited them when the invaders came. They faced a difficult dilemma. Should they stand and fight, joining the Home Guard or regular army units to man the defences and falling back to the stop lines with the main defence force, or, since the police service was a civilian organisation, was it their duty to remain behind? Should they stay with the civilian population, letting the battle roll over them, in order to serve and protect their communities just as they had always done?

The Chief Constable of Maidstone, in common with his contemporaries around the country, issued instructions to his men that should the German invaders come, it was not the job of the police to fight them.

They were not to engage the enemy in any way whatsoever, but were to do their best to look after the civilians in their area. This was entirely in accord with official instructions issued by the Ministry of Information, the War Office and the Ministry of Home Security, which advised civilians not already evacuated to 'stay put'. The great fear was that refugees fleeing from the fighting would clog the roads, as had happened in northern Europe, and it was vital that roads be kept clear for the movement of troops and supplies.

On 14 July 1940 an announcement in *The Times* described how an ordinary person should react if fighting were to break out nearby:

> I remember that this is the moment to act like a soldier. I do not get panicky. I stay put. I do not say: 'I must get out of here.'

I remember that fighting men must have clear roads. I do not go on to the road on a bicycle, in a car or on foot. Whether I am at work or at home I just stay put.

There were also far darker warnings, including this snippet that appeared under the heading, 'What will happen to me if I don't stay put?':

> If you do not stay put you will stand a very good chance of being killed. The enemy may machine-gun you from the air inorderto increase your panic, or you may run into enemy forces, which have landed behind you.

Prime Minister Winston Churchill made many rousing speeches about Britons defending their homeland, including:

LEFT: *An RAF anti-aircraft gunner in an armoured car, Hastings, March 1943. This would have been a familiar sight to residents during the war.*

'...we shall fight on the beaches, we shall fight on the landing grounds, we shall fight in the fields and in the streets...' in June 1940, and 'We shall defend every village, every town and every city. The vast mass of London alone, fought street by street, could easily devour an entire hostile army...' in the July. But Churchill's speeches were intended to boost morale, impress the Americans and worry the Germans more than they were to be taken as direct instructions.

Police orders intimated that civilians who had not already been evacuated were to stay where they were and that officers would be expected to keep the roads clear for military movements, preventing civilian refugees from crowding the highways – by force, if necessary. Some provisions were made for evacuating strategic areas known as 'nodal points', where it was felt that the enemy could be held for a time. Police designated roads in such areas for the use of either the military or for evacuees, and police officers were to be stationed along the way to keep the civilians on their designated routes. Despite the fear of general panic in such a situation, the officers would not have been armed, although the government had decided in May 1940 that the police were to carry firearms and act as a kind of secondary Home Guard. There were never sufficient weapons available for this plan to be put into effect, however, and police officers (unless on special duties) remained unarmed throughout the course of the war. The situation for any police officer in Foyle's position would have been extremely perplexing. Ultimately, it was left pretty much to the discretion of the individual whether to get out of an occupied area, should the opportunity present itself, or whether to stay behind to try to keep order in an area occupied by the Germans.

While it seems unimaginable that, had there been a prolonged occupation, British

ABOVE: *A British police officer gives directions to a German sailor on Jersey during the German occupation of the Channel Islands.*

THE ROLE OF THE POLICE IN WARTIME | 25

police officers could ever have worked under German military authorities, in one part of the British Isles that is exactly what happened. The Channel Islands were occupied by the Germans from 30 June 1940 until the Germans on the islands surrendered on 9 May 1945. The islands were taken without a fight, having been demilitarised by the British, who believed that the close proximity to the French mainland would make the islands almost impossible to defend or resupply. They were also regarded as being of little strategic significance. Once the decision to let the islands fall into German hands was made, 30,000 people, mainly children and those of the island's Jewish community, were evacuated. This represented less than a third of the total population.

Police officers who remained on the islands found that their role changed significantly. They had to suffer the humiliation of being forced to salute German officers, or face being prosecuted and fined, and had to attempt to walk the fine line between co-operation and collaboration. For some this meant 'forgetting' to go out on patrol at night and leaving the Germans to enforce their own curfew regulations, or ignoring those who kept forbidden radios unless an informant, of which there were many, made it impossible for them not to. Old scores that vindictive islanders thought they could settle by denouncing neighbours to the police for infringement of new German regulations often got no further than the officer to whom the complaint was made, although if a German official became involved the police were obliged to take action.

In many ways the Channel Islands police acted as a buffer between the Germans and the civilian population when it came to maintaining law and order. But there was no way that all contact between the Germans

and the locals could be avoided, there being almost twice as many Germans as there were islanders. The Germans appropriated accommodation and confiscated property as they saw fit and the police were powerless to intervene. One unofficial police rule, however, served to cover common thefts committed on the islands. Stealing from another islander was taken very seriously. Should a police officer discover someone stealing from the Germans, on the other hand, who could blame him for looking the other way?

Had the Germans invaded mainland Britain, the police would have had little choice but to try to carry on policing their patch as they had done before. The German authorities would have dealt most severely with any crimes committed against them, the army and the Gestapo hunting down saboteurs or dissidents, but the police would have carried on dealing with domestic disputes, burglaries and other 'civil' crimes. The alternative would have been to allow the German military a free reign, exposing the populace to the harshest of treatment. If a policeman viewed his duty as being 'to protect and serve' then he might well have wanted to try to help maintain some kind of order under German rule.

In the end, police officers on the mainland never had to make the decision between keeping the peace and becoming a combatant unless, of course, they chose to volunteer for military service. When war was declared in 1939, those in the police service were deemed to be in a 'reserved occupation'. These were the jobs that were considered vital to the war effort and workers categorised as such included miners, shipyard workers and those working in the aircraft industry. The list of those jobs designated as reserved occupations grew as the war progressed until there were tens of thousands, but initially the regulations were not too strictly enforced. Men of military age with essential industrial skills did disappear into military service in the early recruitment rush and the police service lost more than its fair share of personnel. Police officers who were young and fit, well disciplined and used to being in uniform were prime candidates for recruitment to the armed forces. Many were also former soldiers, still on the military reserve list and first to be called up to return to their former units.

Since 1936, when the prospect of war with Germany began to look like a possibility, the Home Office began preparing the police for a wartime role. The first circulars regarding air raids had been sent to local authorities the previous year. But mindful of the effects that air raids were having on the civilian population in the Spanish Civil War, the Home Office requested that selected police officers from each area be given special air raid precaution training. The police were expected to play a major role in establishing and co-ordinating all forms of civil defence and they were essential to the recruitment and training of the Air Raid Wardens Service established in 1937. Police duties in civil defence were just one new area with which they would have to cope. Chief Constables all over the country began to contemplate the effect that a major conflict would have on their resources. Some estimates predicted that the extra responsibilities the police would have to undertake would require three times the regular number of officers. In fact, the police service began losing staff to the armed forces as soon as war was declared, immediately facing a severe manpower shortage.

The police authorities were forced to call in their reserves, returning retired officers to active duties. There was also a second reserve of Special Constables, part-time unpaid volunteer policemen who would now be expected to play a greater role in policing their communities, being permitted to take on paid, full-time employment with the police. Many of these volunteers, however, might themselves become unavailable due to military service and many more part-timers had to be recruited from among the able-bodied men in reserved occupations. In addition, there was also a Police War Reserve consisting of men over the age of 25 who volunteered for police service rather than joining the armed forces. These were paid full-time officers who had no prior police experience and needed to be trained quickly.

To these were added the Women's Auxiliary Police Corps. There were very few female police officers in service at the outbreak of World War II, although the Metropolitan Police in London had established their Women Police Patrols in 1918, and some forces recruited no female auxiliaries at all during the war. Despite this, there were 10,000 WAPC volunteers in service nationwide before the war ended, although they were given no police powers, being employed only as clerical staff, telephonists or drivers. More volunteers came in the form of the Police Auxiliary Messenger Service – young men between the ages of 15 and 18, who volunteered on a part-time basis ostensibly to use their own bicycles to deliver urgent messages. In some cases, however, the youngsters were pressed into manning the police switchboards, quite a responsibility given that almost all police communications at the time went via their own telephone networks.

Police switchboards were linked to the famous police boxes strategically placed on beat officer's patrol routes. These boxes, familiar to anyone who has ever watched the television series *Dr Who*, were little more than sentry boxes and acted as temporary

ABOVE: *Mrs Russell, a volunteer in the Women's Auxiliary Police Corps in Preston, attends to her make-up. By the end of the war there were 10,000 WAPC volunteers.*

ABOVE: *In the 1940s, the police had no radios and the telephones housed in the police boxes scattered around Britain's cities were a vital link in their communications networks.*

bases out on the streets for officers whose beats took them far from their home stations. Aside from providing a convenient place for a bobby to hang his overcoat on a warm day, the important thing was that the boxes were equipped with a telephone, allowing incidents to be reported by the general public as well as police patrols. In the 1940s the police officer's only other means of calling for assistance was his whistle. A few shrill blasts would bring other officers running from neighbouring beats. Personal radios for police officers were as much a part of science fiction at that time as *Dr Who*'s police box would later become. In fact, most police forces did not equip their officers with the new, cumbersome, limited-range walkie-talkies until about the same time as *Dr Who* first disguised his TARDIS as a police box in the 1960s.

The Metropolitan Police first experimented with radios in vehicles on Epsom Downs in 1920, but Brighton Police claim to be first to bring in widespread use of radios in 1933. Throughout the 1930s various forces tried out radios in vans, cars and even motorcycle-sidecar combinations. For the most part, however, a bobby on the beat, or detectives like Foyle and Paul Milner, out visiting a crime scene, had to rely on police boxes or the public telephone system to keep in touch with the station. Inevitably, this meant that making their enquiries took far longer.

When the war began, of course, the priority for the country's chief constables was not improving communications, but increasing manpower. Recruitment and training was a huge undertaking. Between 1939 and 1945 in London alone around 20,000 men became Police Reservists with the Metropolitan Police. Naturally, the Met required more recruits than any other

force but there were 179 separate police authorities in Britain in 1939 (today there are less than 50), each major town running its own force. The struggling ranks of ageing officers, raw recruits, enthusiastic volunteers and teenagers soon found themselves facing a major administrative nightmare. On 14 May 1940, Secretary of War Anthony Eden announced on the radio that a new defence force consisting of men of all ages 'not at present engaged in military service' was being established. 'Now is your opportunity,' Mr Eden encouraged his listeners. 'We want all men who are British subjects, between the ages of 15 and 65, to come forward now and offer their services...'

To where was this army of 'Local Defence Volunteers', later known as the Home Guard, expected to come forward? To the local police station of course. Unfortunately, many local police stations had no idea that 'Dad's Army' was on its way, and some form of registration system had to be swiftly devised. But it was not swift enough. The first volunteer showed up at 'Foyle's' station in Hastings before Eden's radio broadcast had actually ended. He was soon followed by 800 others. Across the country, more than 250,000 men volunteered within the next 24 hours.

The experience of having helped set up the ARP stood the police in good stead when it came to dealing with the queues of recruits, but as soon as a local LDV commander was appointed the police gratefully relinquished the responsibility. To an extent they were still involved in vetting applicants. But with the LDV's ranks having swollen to 1.5 million by July 1940, it was not uncommon for the police to see the local poacher or a dockyard worker with a penchant for burglary march past in the street, in uniform and carrying a loaded firearm.

ABOVE: *Police officers were often first on the scene at bomb sites after, or even during, an air raid. Here policemen and other rescue workers swarm over the wreckage of a junior school in Liverpool.*

In the course of their duties during the war police officers attended the sites of bomb blasts during and after air raids. They worked with the Home Guard and the other Civil Defence organisations to search for survivors in shattered buildings, secure the scene as best they could and identify unexploded bombs. In some areas in the early part of the war, the police were also the local fire fighters. Most regions, however, had a fairly well-drilled ARP team. With the ARP Act of 1938, the government had forced local authorities to make provision for the establishment of teams of wardens, first aid posts, emergency ambulances, gas decontamination centres and casualty clearing stations. Naturally, some councils prepared their plans better than others

but the first ARP 'professionals', full-time, salaried personnel, were appointed many months before the outbreak of war.

Most ARP wardens, however, were part-time volunteers. When blackout restrictions were imposed, they patrolled the streets at night looking for any chink of light showing through the heavy drapes that everyone hung at their windows. Any such light through the curtains could give a German bomber high overhead something to aim for. But the wardens' famously ferocious call of 'Put that bloody light out!' was one of the few weapons he had in his arsenal. Persistent offenders or anyone refusing to obey his polite instruction had to be reported to the police. A police officer was then required to charge the miscreant, but falling foul of the law may not have been what a blackout offender dreaded most. In Hastings they were regularly 'named and shamed' in the *Hastings & St Leonard's Observer*, lists of those whom the police had prosecuted for showing lights from their homes or work premises appearing on the inside pages along with the amount they were fined – usually around 10 shillings. Rather than go to all the trouble of pursuing a conviction and a court case, some officers reportedly opted for direct action, pasting newspaper over people's windows, or even shooting out a visible light bulb with an air gun.

Wardens and police officers were also on the lookout for anyone using an unscreened torch during the blackout or riding a bicycle with unshielded lights, or even just poorly shielded in some instances. Conversely, at Battle Sessions Court, as reported in *The Observer* on 28 September 1940, one police constable gave evidence against cyclist Albert Pack, whom he had arrested for riding a bicycle *without* a red rear light. For this, Mr Pack was fined one shilling.

On Foyle's patch in Hastings, just as in the rest of the country, policemen were hard-pressed to cope with the extra workload directly attributable to the war. In 1940 the Deputy Chief Constable, Superintendent Buddle, found himself in court giving evidence in the case of six boys and a girl who broke into a Hastings photographic store, stealing a camera and causing £50 worth of damage to a window and shuttering. Mr Buddle testified that the children were of good character, although some were refugees who had been placed with foster families in the area. The foster parents, furthermore, were the ones who had alerted him to the fact that the youngsters were responsible for the break-in, while assuring him that the children was essentially well behaved. Each of the culprits was put on probation for a year.

In July 1940 the government announced that residents in coastal towns around the country were to observe a strict curfew during the blackout hours. No one was allowed on the streets from half an hour after sunset to half an hour before sunrise without a special permit. In September 1940 the first person to be arrested by the Hastings police for flouting the curfew was Maud Guild, who was charged with being in East Parade in contravention of Defence Regulations at 10.40 pm and further convicted of being drunk and disorderly. She might have got away with it at the time, had she had not become hysterical when asked to go home. Maud was fined £1 for defying the curfew with a further £1 for being drunk and disorderly, and allowed a month to pay.

A gardener in Hastings was arrested under the Control of Photography Order and fined £10 for photographing the ruins of bombed buildings without permission. Far from being a spy out to pass on evidence of the effects of the Luftwaffe's bombing campaign, he was actually a keen photographer who had taken pictures of the same buildings before the war and wanted shots of them in ruins to contrast with his earlier snaps. At the same time, crimes large and small, breathtakingly stupid and frustratingly complex, continued to swell the buff folders piled on detectives' desks. In early January 1940 Inspector Small of Hastings Police gave evidence in the trial of Reginald Wiggins. He was accused of attempting to steal a stove from Cosens store in Lower South Road, having apparently tried to walk out of the shop with it in broad daylight while staff were otherwise engaged.

The *Hastings & St Leonard's Observer* reported on 6 January 1940 that Detective Sergeant Copper (the fictional Sergeant Milner somehow has a far more believable

ABOVE: *Home Secretary Sir John Gilmour opens the Metropolitan Police Laboratory at Hendon in 1935.*

name) had arrested a trolley bus conductor called Maurice Lee Roberts for obtaining money under false pretences from Jessie Ethel Standing, a divorced mother-of-five. Roberts had befriended one of Standing's children, who took the bus to school every day, and subsequently came to know the boy's mother, learning that she owned several properties and a number of Woolworth's shares. Over a period of two years he attempted to interest her in several business ventures, including opening a hotel and a private school, convincing her that he himself owned some 800 acres of farmland and coal mines in Wales. Roberts claimed he was

actually a member of the Secret Service and only working on the buses in order to root out spies and fifth columnists. He managed to persuade his victim to part with £166 2s 6d, which may not sound much today, but at that time the average wage for a skilled labourer on a building site was less than £1 per week and even someone in a relatively well-paid job might only be earning £3 or £4 per week.

Even before the real wartime shortages kicked in, before rationing took hold and before the black marketeers began turning the war to their advantage, the police in places like Hastings had their hands full. But what modern crime-fighting techniques could they rely on to help solve a case? They were without radios and mobile phones were undreamed of, but the police still had a few tricks up their sleeves when it came to the study of evidence. In several episodes of *Foyle's War*, Sergeant Milner refers to having found, or not found, fingerprints at a crime scene. But how much use was fingerprint evidence at that time?

The use of fingerprint identification in the 1940s was actually a well-established technique. The fact that fingerprints existed, even that they were unique to an individual, had been known for many centuries. Legal documents in ancient Babylon and China are even believed to have been authenticated with a thumb print as well as a signature. Many scientists carried out research into fingerprints, but it wasn't until the nineteenth century that a classification system was developed that allowed effective comparison of different prints. All over the world interest in the new technique was shown and in 1892 a bloody fingerprint was used to convict a murderer in Buenos Aires. In 1901 the Fingerprint Department at New Scotland Yard was set up, with a burglary in 1902 becoming the first criminal conviction to be won in the UK using fingerprint evidence. The first use of fingerprints to secure a murder conviction in Britain was in 1905, when Alfred and Albert Stratton were hanged after Alfred's prints were found on a cash box in the Deptford shop where the owners, Mr and Mrs Farrow, had been killed.

By World War II, therefore, fingerprints were a highly prized item of evidence, although the identification of prints could not be achieved nearly as quickly as it can today. Unlike a modern detective, Sergeant Milner would not have been able to have a set of prints run through a computer database. The first electronic computer, Colossus, was not built until 1943 and was top secret,

being used at Bletchley Park for cracking German codes. It took up a whole room and was a huge achievement, although 60 years on it could easily be out-performed by a modern laptop. Milner would, however, have been able to have fingerprints from a crime scene compared with those of a suspect, or with those held on an index card system – a laborious, time-consuming process. But fingerprints were not the only forensic evidence of use as experts had been providing scenes-of-crime evidence analysis for many years.

In 1816 a murderer in Warwick was caught when an impression left in the earth was matched up to a patch on a pair of his trousers. Then, in 1884, a scrap of paper taken from a gunshot victim's head wound was matched to the wadding used in a pistol and the newspaper found in the suspected murderer's pocket. Inspector Arthur Walls was shot and killed while attending a burglary in Eastbourne in 1912. His murderer, George Mackay, was convicted after a gunsmith took wax casts of the rifling in the barrel of Mackay's revolver, proving that the rounds which killed Inspector Walls had come from that weapon.

The techniques of forensic science were, in fact, progressing at an amazing rate by the outbreak of World War II. Microscopes could be used, for example, to compare scratches left by tools at a crime scene, and in 1935 the Forensic Science Laboratory opened at the Police College in Hendon. How many of the new methods would have been available to Foyle and Milner? The answer, especially as the war began to dominate every aspect of life in Britain and resources grew increasingly scarce, was precious few. Instead, they would have had to rely on exhaustive witness statements, their own powers of observation, intelligent deduction and, of course, good old-fashioned leg work.

2. CRIME & PUNISHMENT

The notion that during World War II the people of Britain stood shoulder-to-shoulder, digging for victory in their vegetable plots, working long shifts in factories or serving with loyalty and patriotism in the armed forces is a somewhat flawed concept. While the vast majority of people did, of course, do their duty to the very best of their ability their idea of precisely what duty entailed might not always have been in absolute harmony with that of the authorities. Laws were broken and the police kept busy – but what might be seen as a wartime crime wave should be viewed in context. There were far more laws to break, after all, than ever before.

On 24 August 1939 Parliament passed the Emergency Powers (Defence) Act which brought into play the wartime Defence Regulations as well as giving the government wide-ranging powers to commandeer property and land for military use. Ordinary people were obliged to move out of their homes or give up their farmland for the creation of live firing ranges or airfields, just as happened to farmer David Barrett in the Foyle's War episode 'Invasion'. While Barrett was justifiably upset that his land was being ruined by the building of the air base, he was but one man. An entire community of 3,000 people was uprooted from an area of 25 square miles around Slapton Sands in Dorset, where the beaches were deemed ideal as training grounds for the D-Day landings. You were liable to be arrested if you tried to return to your own home after having been relocated. For those whose lives were directly affected in this way, the Defence Regulations were especially hard to bear, but no one was completely immune from their influence.

ABOVE: *This watercolour by Dwight C. Shepler, The US Navy's official combat artist, shows why the residents of Slapton Sands had to be relocated as the area was used to train troops for the D-Day landings.*

What the Defence Regulations brought with them was an avalanche of new offences for which you could be prosecuted. Prior to their introduction, you could, either deliberately or unwittingly, with guilt or in innocence, be arrested for any one of around 300,000 offences in England and Wales – although even the most dedicated criminal would have to work fairly hard to fit all of them in before he retired. By the end of the war, new laws meant that number had risen to almost 480,000. Pursuing ordinary citizens for flouting curfews or contravening blackout regulations (300,000 blackout offences were prosecuted in 1940) added to the police's ever-growing workload and made the forces of law and order extremely unpopular. In some areas, jailing miners for contravening the new regulations by going on strike didn't help in that respect, either. Before the war, to almost everyone the police had been seen as friendly faces, but now there a change of attitude was afoot. Now even the most respectable of citizens could find themselves falling foul of the law, caught in contravention of any number of new regulations.

In a country like Britain, where most considered themselves to be honest, upright citizens and even a hint of impropriety scandalised the middle-class suburbs, breaking the law was not something that ordinary people would normally contemplate. When food rationing was introduced in January 1940, however, breaking the law – or what might have been seen as 'bending the rules' – came to be regarded as part of survival. Rationing had been a fact of life almost from the outset of the war with petrol having been restricted since September 1939, although at that time most people did not own cars so petrol rationing affected the general public far less than the clothes rationing that began in June 1941.

The first foods to be rationed were butter, lard, sugar, bacon and ham, but almost every other foodstuff, including meat, was to follow. Rationing was administered by the Ministry of Food, which had 50,000 civil servants involved in the distribution of ration books and the registering and monitoring of authorised outlets. Each family or individual was issued with a ration book and then had to register for food items with their local grocer, baker and butcher. The Ministry of Food then ensured that the shopkeepers received enough supplies to cater for their registered customers. When his customers bought their sugar or bacon, the shopkeeper took the ration coupons or marked up the ration book to show that the approved rations had changed hands. At least, that was how it was supposed to work.

If muddling through as best you could involved paying a little more for a few extra slices of ham, or buying the odd lipstick from

a dodgy bloke on a street corner (even if it did cost twice the normal price), where was the harm, really? When shortages really began to bite, with Britain's pre-war annual average of 55 million tons of food imports dropping to just 30.5 million tons in 1941 as Germany's U-boats took their toll on trans-Atlantic shipping, people found that the local grocer and butcher often couldn't supply even their basic rations. The result was that, when the opportunity arose, people bought what they could, where they could. With so many people prepared to try to circumvent the system or supplement their rations by buying goods from unlicensed sources without having to use their ration books, the black market flourished. Once established, and with rationing extended to cover all manner of goods, black marketeers had a field day. Their customers, of course, knew better than to to ask the origins of their goods.

LEFT: *Rationing made life tough but when shortages really began to bite, finding even basic foodstuffs could be difficult. When people heard that shops had fresh stock, queues quickly formed, as at this fishmongers in London's Elephant and Castle.*

One meat scam in Liverpool involved the Ministry of Food distribution supervisor Donald Shaw. Shaw's patch was in Warrington, but he and his accomplices had developed an entire supply chain that started at the docks on Merseyside. The truck driver on Shaw's team paid off the clerk supervising the loading of his vehicle. It was detailed as having been loaded with 50 carcasses of beef and lamb from a refrigerated cargo ship. In fact, the clerk allowed dockers to carry on loading the truck until it was eventually driven away with 70 carcasses. The driver then delivered his load to the official distribution centre where, strictly according to the paperwork, 50 carcasses were unloaded. His 20-carcass extra load was immediately whisked away to be delivered to a contact. Five ships were targeted in this way and over 2,000 carcasses, then worth more than £5,000, disappeared onto the black market. The gang was uncovered when the police received complaints from members of the public about a Liverpool butcher, William Eales, who did not always appear to be playing by the ration-book rules. Detectives kept watch on Eales and, when he was ultimately arrested, he spilled the beans on the rest of the gang. He and Shaw were sentenced to four years' penal servitude (a hard labour sentence of anything between three years and life imposed on those whose crimes would previously have merited being transported to a penal colony in, for example, Australia). The driver and his friend (the clerk at the docks) each received three years' penal servitude and two others went to prison for 18 months.

Britain's dockyards had always been an Aladdin's cave of opportunity for both casual thieves and professional gangs. Those who worked aboard cargo ships, laboured on the wharfs or in the handling yards all knew that goods arriving at the port generally had a little extra added to the consignment when it left the manufacturer or supplier to cover

'pilferage' en route. The extra was costed into the price of the goods and if there was no pilfering the end result was that the recipient of the consignment got more than he bargained for and made a tasty profit. To avoid the pilfering of footwear, for many

ABOVE: *Dockyard pilfering was already endemic before the war, making them an irresistible target for black marketeers once wartime restrictions meant that there was a profit to be made on almost everything subject to rationing or in short supply.*

years the army sent boots in consignments that were either all left- or right-footed! Such petty larceny, and the fact that it was known that there were those working at the docks who were prepared to take risks, made the dockyards a magnet for black marketeers.

In early 1942 a wharf superintendent in London was discovered working with two lorry drivers to supply a black market gang. One load intercepted by the police included over 100 boxes of dried fruit and 30 containers of canned meat.

Just like goods travelling by ship, those transported by train were liable to pilfering, although a new phenomenon developed when the railways came under attack from the Luftwaffe. During air raids, when everyone had taken cover, organised gangs would take advantage of the reduced security to raid rail shipments, risking their lives to make off with whatever they could lay their hands on. By 1943 more than £1 million of goods (equivalent to at least £40 million today) had been stolen from the railways and by the end of 1944 it was to be around double that amount. Employees of the railway companies, even engine drivers who had what was regarded as quite a prestigious job, were on low wages compared to other industries. Supplementing their incomes with a little larceny now and again was seen by some to be a perk of the job. One carriage cleaner in Manchester became known to the police as something of a cigarette baron, offering cartons of cigarettes for sale at knock-down prices on a regular basis. His technique for acquiring his stock was quite simple. When he finished work at night, he took a good look around the station platform. Cartons of cigarettes were regularly left stacked on trolleys waiting to be loaded onto a train. He would either help himself to a few cartons, or alternatively wheel the whole trolley down the platform, looking for all the world as if that was his job, out of the station and into the blacked-out street. It was then just a case of pushing the trolley home.

Cigarettes were never actually rationed, but shopkeepers often had to impose their own limits on customers as stocks ran low. Since almost everyone smoked in those days, there was always a ready market for cigarettes. Countless millions of cigarettes found their way onto the black market as organised thieves targeted factories, one gang spending at least two nights in April 1940 dismantling part of a warehouse wall in Kingston-on-Thames under cover of the blackout. They made good their handiwork to the extent that it would not be noticed during the day and used the sound of bombs dropping on London to mask the noise of their nocturnal efforts from patrolling security guards. Their escape route involved carrying their haul over three suburban garden walls to a waiting van in which they ultimately made off with 820,000 cigarettes. Altogether less effort was expended by a cigarette thief in Peckham not too long after the Kingston raid. He simply followed a delivery van through the streets and waited until the driver was busy dropping off a load. Then he jumped into the van and drove off with almost 1.5 million cigarettes worth around £5,000. Gangs who didn't want the hassle of having to get rid of an unwanted truck simply followed the delivery driver in their car and waited for him to disappear into a shop with a consignment. Then they grabbed as many cartons of cigarettes as they could from the back of the truck, flung them in their car and drove off.

When such large quantities of goods went missing, it was inevitable that organised gangs of criminals were involved, if not in the actual theft, then certainly in the disposal of the booty. Every major city had its own crime bosses, its own gangland. In 1930s Glasgow there were The Bridgeton Billy Boys, a loose alliance of hundreds of men (and women) who followed gang leader Billy Fullerton, taking their name in part from his, and in part from William of Orange. Like other Scottish cities, Glasgow's gangland, in common with its schools and football clubs, was divided along sectarian lines. The Protestant Billy Boys' great rivals were a Catholic group from around the Norman Street area known as The Norman Conks. Their clashes were extremely violent affairs, scores of combatants arming themselves with cut-throat razors to do battle in the streets. Glasgow's Chief Constable Percy Sillitoe even sent in mounted police to deal with some confrontations.

Birmingham had the Brummagem Boys, led by Billy Kimber, although many of his followers actually came from south London. Leeds, Sheffield, Bristol, Manchester, Liverpool and Newcastle also all had their own criminal 'royalty' but it was, inevitably, London that was the crime capital of the UK. Perhaps the most influential of London crime bosses were the Sabinis. Years after the war, the infamous Kray twins (then teenagers) appeared before a judge after a fracas and the judge warned them not to go around acting as if they were the Sabinis. Darby and Harry Sabini's enterprises were centred not only around the bars and clubs in London, but extended all over the country via the racecourses, where they ran extortion and protection rackets and gambling scams. But their income from the horse and dog racing meetings was badly affected when both were curtailed during the war years. Their criminal activities were further inconvenienced when, being of Italian extraction, they were interned as enemy aliens, even though Darby's son was killed while serving with the RAF. Other faces in the London underworld included Alf White from King's Cross, the Wood brothers of Bethnal Green, the Elephant Boys from the Elephant and Castle, Arthur Scurry of West Ham (who was known as 'The King of the Gypsies') as well as Jack Spot and Billy Hill.

It didn't take long for Britain's hardcore criminal fraternity to realise the opportunities unfolding before them as the war progressed. Raids on food stores or clothing shipments were commonplace and, initially, many of the official stores were not well guarded. As well as purloining the actual goods, however, there was a healthy trade in ration books.

ABOVE: *Billy Hill was one of the wartime kings of the London underworld, involved in everything from dealing in stolen ration books to armed robbery.*

Ration books and coupons proved easy to forge, but even easier to steal. At the small end of the scale, ration books could be stolen from handbags, or during house burglaries. They could even be acquired from people who would claim that they had lost them due to 'enemy action' during a bombing raid and would be issued with new books or coupons. The big money, however, came when the books and coupons were stolen in bulk. At Romford in 1944, 100,000

No. **EA** 384793

THIS BOOK IS THE PROPERTY OF HIS MAJESTY'S GOVERNMENT

FIRST MONTH

MOTOR SPIRIT RATION BOOK

Private Motor Car or Motor Cycle
(Including Tricycle)

HP 13-15

Registered Number of Vehicle

A ʌ E 328

Date and Office of Issue

NEW MALDEN SURREY — 15 SP 39

The issue of a Ration Book does not guarantee to the holder any minimum quantity of motor spirit and the book may be cancelled at any time without notice.

This book must be surrendered with any unused coupons when application is made for a subsequent book and no such book will be issued unless this book has been surrendered.

ABOVE: *A ration book for petrol issued to a private individual at New Malden in Surrey in 1939. By 1942 even the meagre allowance for private motoring would be reduced to zero and those who were not 'essential' car users tucked their cars away in garages for the duration of the war.*

complete ration books, reportedly worth around £500,000 to the thieves, went missing from a ministry office.

Frankie Fraser, who had worked for the Sabinis before the war, was involved in a clothing coupon robbery from Braintree Town Hall in Essex in 1944. A burglar's work was made far easier during the blackouts as there were no street lights and no lights on the exterior of buildings to illuminate anyone up to no good. Someone, however, spotted Frank and his friends, and the police were after them as soon as they exited the building. They made off in a van stolen specifically for the job, heading for their own stomping ground south of the Thames where they thought they would stand more of a chance of shaking off their pursuers. Unfortunately for them, the van ran out of petrol halfway through the Rotherhithe Tunnel. Stealing a van, it appears, was no problem, but fuel rationing meant that stealing one with enough petrol in it for the job was far more difficult. Perhaps they should have gone for petrol rather than clothing coupons.

Although the private motorist had been permitted a small allowance when petrol was rationed in 1939, by 1942 the use of private cars for pleasure was banned completely. The entertainer Ivor Novello was imprisoned in 1944 for contravening the fuel regulations. Novello had had his Rolls-Royce converted to run on gas rather than petrol, with a huge bag of gas bulging in a crate on the roof, although a little petrol was still needed to get the engine going. He had applied for permission to use the car to travel to and from the theatre when he was appearing in the West End in *The Dancing Years,* but was refused. But he got round the ban when a friend suggested that he 'give' the car to the company for which she worked. Her firm would then apply for an essential user's licence that would enable them to get petrol for the car and Novello could continue to drive it – or rather, be driven in it, as he employed a chauffeur. The scam was soon exposed and Novello was prosecuted and spent a month in jail.

Trading in ration coupons was forbidden, even if you had come by the coupons perfectly legitimately. If you didn't like butter, but wanted some extra bacon, the easiest thing to do was to swap with a friend or another member of your family. You swapped the actual bacon or butter, of course, not the coupons. Even then you could end up on the wrong side of the law. Hoarding food was an offence under the Acquisition of Food (Excessive Quantities) Order. Officials were empowered to come into your home and go through your larder to ensure you had no more than a week's food ration on your shelves.

Trying to buy extra rations using more coupons than you were supposed to have could also land you in hot water. As Provost Marshal of Great Britain (head of the Military Police) and a former Assistant Commissioner of the Metropolitan Police, Major General Sir Percy Laurie really should have known better than to try fiddling the ration-book system. He was caught in possession of two ration books, one issued to him as a civilian and one military book. Sir Percy's assertion that he thought he needed one for day-to-day use and the military book for when he was travelling was made all the more incredible when it was revealed that he had discussed having his servant sent abroad so that he would be unable to testify in court. Sir Percy was fined £550 and, had his term as Provost not been almost over, he would surely have been dismissed.

Of far greater concern to the police than the fact that members of the public, even prominent ones, were defrauding the rationing system, was that government officials clearly had to be in league with criminals when it came to the major thefts from ministry offices. So many new officials had been recruited as administrators and in clerical positions that only the most basic of checks could be made on their backgrounds. If they were recommended by the Labour Exchange and turned up with the appropriate paperwork and references, that was usually good enough to get them the job. Because of this, crime gangs found it relatively easy to place members of their own organisations in positions of influence, and opportunist criminals could scarcely believe their luck.

In 1942 the Admiralty put Vincent Furlong in charge of some of its equipment stores in the North of England and soon came to regret it. A number of items went missing before Furlong finally purloined 15,000 batteries worth around £3,000. It transpired that he had been released from prison just two months before the Navy put him in charge of its storage depots. He was sentenced to five years' penal servitude.

ABOVE: *As these London housewives queue to buy their meagre meat rations, most would have heard how readily available it was on the black market for those willing to pay the price, although few would have been able to afford it.*

In 1943 Leonard Blake, the Food Executive Officer at Barking Food Control Office, was convicted of issuing false permits to a number of grocers in the area, giving them the opportunity to purchase ten times the amount of sugar to which they were entitled. This kept their legitimate customers well supplied and left them with surplus stocks to sell on to black market contacts. Blake was paid handsomely by the grocers for issuing the permits, but his ultimate reward was three years' penal servitude.

One female Food Enforcement Officer, who worked at the Brighton Food Office based in the Royal Pavilion, was also a fire watcher, stationed on the roof of the building at night. One night in August 1942, she broke into a colleague's office while supposedly on

fire duty, forced open a locked cabinet and stole 80,000 clothing coupons. She attempted to sell the coupons to women in clubs and dance halls in Brighton before looking to London to dispose of the bulk of her haul. An intermediary set up a meeting with two 'buyers' in a London hotel. The buyers turned out to be Scotland Yard detectives and the Food Enforcement Officer spent the next three years in penal servitude.

Seeing a member of the Food Control Office fall from grace in such a way would have brought smiles of satisfaction to some people's faces. The job of those who worked in the Food Control Office involved checking up on traders in shops or restaurants to ensure they were complying with all of the regulations. The government set maximum prices for most items and it was an offence for a trader to charge more. Like the grocers who acquired extra sugar supplies from Leonard Blake, restaurant owners attempting to get their hands on more than their fair share of food were also breaking the law. The proprietor of the Elite Café in East Grinstead was prosecuted in 1943 for supplying false figures to the Ministry of Food. Businesses such as cafés were awarded points based on the number of meals served on the premises. The more meals served, the greater number of points accumulated, and the more food would be allocated in future based on the points total. Food Control officials kept watch on the café, having suspected that the owner was fiddling the system. A note was taken of the number of customers actually served on the premises and compared to the number the owner claimed to have served. The café owner was found to be claiming almost three times as many points as he was entitled to and was fined £5 with 10 guineas costs.

Crooked businessmen were not the only ones to try to turn a profit from the misfortunes of war. During The Blitz in London, a scam was very quickly in operation whereby an unfortunate resident would turn up at the local National Assistance office claiming their home had been destroyed in the previous night's raid. A genuine claimant was entitled to receive cash payments to cover necessities and give the 'bombed-out' family a chance to make ends meet until they could get back on their feet. The system was open to abuse as, at the height of The Blitz, it was impossible for officials to check every address to make sure that the claimant's home had actually been blown up. Sometimes the areas worst affected by the bombing would still be inaccessible anyway. A claimant could also expect to receive a new identity card and ration book if he or she maintained the documents had been lost in the blast. All of this assistance was vital to those who actually needed it – for a few, it was just another

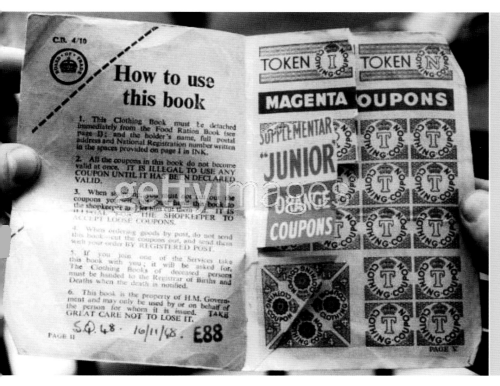

LEFT: *Ration books of clothing coupons like this one were highly prized both by organised criminals and opportunist thieves, such was their value on the black market.*

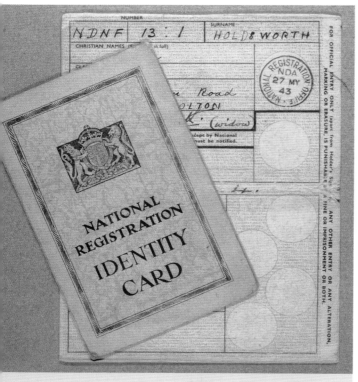

ABOVE: *Everyone was required to carry an identity card like this one during the war and had to show the card to any police officer or military official when asked. Failing to do so could mean being fined, imprisoned, or both.*

had to be prepared to produce it for a police officer, or a member of the military when asked so to do. Setting aside the fact that a draft dodger or a deserter would have no ration book and be unable to buy food, walking the streets without an ID card was a very risky business. The military police from all branches of the services worked with the civilian police to round up deserters, carrying out spot checks at race courses, football matches, cinemas, restaurants and dance halls. In London's West End in May 1944 police swooped on nightspots and amusement arcades, civilian officers operating alongside military policemen who carried rifles with fixed bayonets. They made many arrests, but certainly never managed fully to control the problem. During the course of the war, around 80,000 men went 'absent without leave' from the army alone.

Some of these absentees, of course, were at large somewhere in Europe. Of those who headed for home, some were hidden by friends or family who faced stiff penalties for harbouring their loved ones. One Brighton man hid under the floorboards of his house for four months after deserting, and his wife and mother were each fined £21 for their part in concealing his presence. Others had little choice but to turn to crime to survive. A few words with the right people in the right pub could see a deserter supplied with a ration book and an ID card that might, perhaps, show him to be one of over 300,000 military personnel discharged as being medically unfit for service.

Once a deserter had made contact with the criminal underworld, he could find himself being made very welcome indeed. He might have some particular skills that a gang would find useful – knowledge of explosives, for example, or he may have been taught to drive heavy goods vehicles. Alternatively, he might be able to supply information about

way of turning a quick profit. One man was sentenced to three years' penal servitude in 1941 after it was discovered that he had made 19 separate claims.

A new or replacement National Registration Identity Card was a commodity that could be traded if you knew the right people. There was a ready market for ID cards, genuine or forged, among the criminal fraternity. Although forgers found ID cards fairly easy to replicate, the true article was always preferable. Anyone living outside the law, avoiding military service, or who had deserted from the armed forces would find it extremely difficult to get by without an ID card and a ration book. From the time they were first issued in September 1939, everyone had to carry their ID card at all times and army stores, the NAAFI service shops and canteens, payroll movements or weapons dumps. A deserter with the right attitude could become a very useful member of the team, easily disappearing into the murky world of organised crime.

Some deserters, however, cast a shadow far darker even than those of the underworld. When James Hagan sent his 15-year-old daughter Mary on a simple errand to the local shop in the Waterloo area of Liverpool in November 1940, little did he know that when she stepped out of the door it would be the last time he saw her alive. Her body was found in a concrete blockhouse near Brook Vale Bridge. She had been raped and strangled. A scrap of army field dressing found near the body led police to believe

they were probably looking for a soldier, and two witnesses said they had seen a man in army uniform standing near the bridge. One even identified the man as Samuel Morgan, absent without leave from the First Battalion of the Irish Guards. Less than two weeks later Morgan was in London when a police constable spotted him acting suspiciously and demanded to see his ID. He ran off, but was arrested after a chase. The field dressing matched that from Morgan's kit and soil samples recovered from his uniform matched those taken from the blockhouse. He was hanged in Liverpool on 9 April 1941.

Another deserter, Canadian soldier Mervin McEwen, took to living in a hut in Savile Park in Halifax. He became friends with 82-year-old Mark Turner and one night

ABOVE: *Hikers in Surrey produce their identity cards for a policeman who, judging by the cycle clips fastening the bottoms of his trousers round his ankles, caught up with them by bike.*

LEFT: *Soldiers and sailors gather round to read a notice hung outside Wandsworth Prison to inform the public of an execution, just as in the case of Ernest Kemp in 1944.*

in April 1943, Turner invited McEwen and another man to his home, where they had a drink together. Turner's guests left around 9.00 pm. The next morning his neighbour was concerned that the old man was not up and about by 11.00 am, long after he usually started his day. His battered body was found when police forced their way into his house. Fingerprints were discovered on a whisky bottle, a lemonade bottle and a glass, and the battle dress uniform of a soldier of the Royal Canadian Corps was also found. Mervin McEwen, however, was nowhere to be seen. Three months later police on a routine enquiry called at the home of Annie Perfect in Manchester. Annie was living with a man calling himself James Acton, but when asked to produce his ID, the card showed him to be Mark Turney, although the officer immediately noticed that the 'y' had been changed to an 'r'. The man was asked to sign his name and wrote 'Mervin Turney'. He was

taken into custody and swiftly identified as Mervin McEwen. Having returned to Turner's house late at night after the old man had gone to sleep, he murdered Mark Turner and stole his ID card. His intention was simply to steal food and drink, but Turner woke up while McEwen was cooking himself a meal and he had beaten Turner to death. McEwen was hanged in Leeds on 3 February 1944.

Sometimes a keen-eyed policeman's attention to the smallest of details could lead to an important arrest. When a railway policeman at St Pancras Station in London saw an army sergeant kissing a member of the WAAF (Women's Auxiliary Air Force) goodbye, it was a scene that must have been acted out hundreds of times that day. But the policeman thought there was something odd about this soldier – he was wearing medal ribbons on his uniform to which he surely could not be entitled. The sergeant, Ernest Kemp, was detained for questioning and found to be a deserter. Clothing coupons in his possession linked him to Iris Deeley, a leading aircraftwoman WAAF, who had been sexually assaulted and strangled in south London a week earlier. The clothing coupons belonged to Iris's fiancé, Kemp having taken them from her after murdering her. Footprints found in the soft earth of the allotment where Iris's body had been discovered also matched Kemp's shoe size. He confessed to the crime and was hanged at Wandsworth Prison on D-Day, 6 June 1944.

During the war years, the values by which so many had previously lived became wildly distorted. Men and women in uniform went through the horrors of seeing friends die in action and for many, not knowing if they were destined to survive the conflict, life became cheap. Among the civilian population, too, it seems that, with death such a constant companion, the idea of taking another's life was no longer as unthinkable as it had been in peacetime. The murder rate soared, and the hangman was kept extremely busy. In the five years up to and including 1939, there had been 55 executions in Britain. Between 1940 and 1945 there were 116.

At that time, the hangman's noose awaited not only those who had committed murder, but also those found guilty of spying, treason, looting or rape. No one was ever hanged for looting, but several rapists were sent to the gallows. Aniceto Martinez, an American soldier, was the last man hanged for rape in Britain prior to capital punishment for the offence being abolished. A guard at a prisoner-of-war camp in Staffordshire, Martinez had left the camp on the night of 6 August 1944 and broken into the home of 75-year-old Agnes Cope at around 3.15 am. He raped the old lady and the next morning she contacted the police. Martinez admitted to the rape after fibres found on his clothes were matched with

samples taken from Cope's bedroom. He died on the gallows at Shepton Mallet on 15 June 1945.

Murder was, however, still the crime that accounted for most executions. Part of the reason behind the increase in the murder rate during the war years was almost certainly the ready availability of firearms. Weapons stolen from military depots, or brought home by soldiers from the battlefields of Europe, became cheap. Army-issue revolvers bought from Canadian soldiers were known to cost as little as £7 but more sophisticated weaponry could be purloined if you knew where to find it. Home Guard weapons stores were not always as secure or well guarded as they ought to have been. Four teenagers, who were armed with sten sub-machine guns and a rifle acquired from a Home Guard Store, robbed the Ambassador cinema in Hayes. Two youths, escaping from a remand home, went on the run with a Tommy gun and 400 rounds of ammunition they stole from a Home Guard depot at Upper Norwood.

Weapons used in murders could, of course, be acquired quite legitimately. In January 1942 Frederick Austin was on leave and spending time with his wife when he 'accidentally' shot her while cleaning his rifle. At Austin's trial, a Home Office scenes-of-crime expert demonstrated that the fatal wound Mrs Austin had suffered could only have been incurred if her husband had held his rifle in the firing position, not if it had gone off accidentally during cleaning. Austin then admitted his wife had found a letter from another woman in his kit bag. He was found guilty of murder and hanged in Bristol in April 1942.

Perhaps the most ghoulish murderer convicted during the war years, however, had no use of firearms. The 'Blackout Ripper,' who stalked the streets of London in 1942, did not receive the kind of publicity that his

ABOVE: *From the spring of 1940 onwards soldiers of the Home Guard patrolled the countryside, creating makeshift guard rooms from places such as this railway station waiting room.*

infamous predecessor had so enjoyed, but he targeted women in much the same way. The fact that there was war news to report and restricted space in the newspapers, which were reduced in size and in the number of pages, meant that the Blackout Ripper's story was not so well publicised.

The killing spree for which Gordon Cummins was eventually convicted began in February 1942, although it is believed he may have murdered two women before then, in October of the previous year. Cummins had been called up in 1941 and joined the RAF. He was billeted in St John's Wood in

London and on 7 February he set out for a night on the town. The next day, 40-year-old Evelyn Hamilton was found strangled and robbed in an air raid shelter. On that same day, Cummins went with prostitute Evelyn Oatley to her flat in central London. Her body was found, strangled and mutilated, three days later. Two days after Evelyn's body was discovered, another prostitute, Margaret Lowe, was also strangled and mutilated, and a fourth woman, Doris Jouannet, met the same gruesome fate. Cummins was only exposed when he attacked a fifth victim the very next day, wining and dining Margaret

Heywood before dragging her into a doorway as they walked through the blacked-out streets and attempting to strangle her. Disturbed by a curious delivery boy, he ran off. In his hurry to get away he dropped his RAF gas mask, which bore his name, rank and serial number.

Undaunted, he then approached prostitute Kathleen Mulcahy, who took him back to her flat where he attacked her. She fought him off and Cummins left, but forgot to take with him his uniform belt. When the attacks were reported, he was easy enough for the police to trace and among his belongings they found souvenirs he had taken from his victims, including cigarette cases and a fountain pen. His fingerprints also matched those recovered at the crime scenes. He was hanged at Wandsworth Prison on 25 June 1942.

While hanging was the ultimate punishment under the law, there were others that have subsequently been abolished but are regularly mentioned in *Foyle's War*, especially when a suspect under questioning is being encouraged to co-operate. A normal prison sentence could be made tougher by including hard labour, which involved physically punishing work. This work was at one time as dispiriting and pointless as it was exhausting. In the nineteenth century hard labour could, for example, involve the 'shot drill'. This was an exercise where prisoners were forced to pick up a cannonball from the ground by stooping without bending the knees, lift it to chest height, move three paces to the left and deposit the ball back on the ground. This could go on for hours on end. The crank machine was another exhausting procedure. Prisoners were made to turn a handle on the side of a wooden box. Inside the handle pushed paddles through a layer of sand. Prison officers could make the handle more difficult to push

by turning a screw, hence the slang term 'screw' for a prison officer. The treadmill was similar to the crank machine. Prisoners held onto a bar or strap and stepped on the blades of a paddle wheel, forcing it round in an exhausting routine that could go on for hours each day.

By the 1930s, penal reform had seen the opening of the first 'open prisons' and criminals were treated in a far more humane manner. Hard labour might involve breaking rocks on Dartmoor rather then the treadmill or crank machine. Hard labour and penal servitude were abolished in 1948.

The rations' scams were to continue long after the war ended, with rationing continuing well into the 1950s. Some foodstuffs, such as flour, had been taken off the rationed list as early as 1948, but others, including meat and bacon, were rationed right up to 1954. Petrol was de-rationed in 1950. Returning servicemen, some greatly traumatised by their experiences, caused major problems for the police in the immediate aftermath of the war. But most respectable civilians who might have been tempted to 'bend the rules' during the war in order to provide for their families were soon back on the straight and narrow. The Defence Regulations, blackouts, curfews and even most of the restricted areas quickly became a thing of the past. Once the beaches were cleared of mines, you could even go for a dip in the sea again.

On Foyle's patch in Hastings, August 1945 saw day trippers flocking to the town at a rate of up to 20,000 a day with 44 hotels, 145 guest houses and 447 bed-and-breakfast businesses fully booked for the August Bank Holiday. The peculiar problems of wartime crime were over and for police officers like Foyle and Milner, the massive influx of holidaymakers would have confirmed that it was back to business as usual.

3. FOYLE, MILNER, SAM & ANDREW

The main characters in *Foyle's War* are very distinct individuals whose speech, dress and mannerisms have all been meticulously researched to recreate the atmosphere of the 1940s as accurately as possible. Sometimes, however, making the recreation too accurate would be detrimental to main aim of the series, which is, of course, to entertain. For example, if everyone in *Foyle's War* spoke exactly as they would have done during the war there would be a grave risk that the language could become impenetrable to a modern audience.

Terry Charman is an historian who works at the Imperial War Museum in London. He advises the *Foyle's War* production team and writer Anthony Horowitz on how people spoke in the 1940s, how they dressed and on how things, in general, were done back then. 'Slang expressions would have been used far more than they are in the series,' says Charman, 'but the truth is that if the language used was to be totally true to the 1940s, we would find it more than a little confusing. Expressions from popular American films were widely used. For example, when someone told you something that was difficult to believe, you might say, sarcastically, "sez you." That's a phrase that does crop up from time to time in *Foyle's War*. Today's equivalent might be "in your dreams," which would seem even more strange to anyone in 1940 than "sez you" is to us today.

'Just like today, people used catchphrases that they picked up from comedy shows. In the 1940s these were radio shows, and *ITMA* (*It's That Man Again*) was the one that everyone listened to.'

ABOVE: *Julian Ovenden, playing Foyle's son Andrew, sits in the cockpit of his Spitfire. Andrew became Sam's 'boyfriend', though he would not have been referred to in that way at the time. Her 'young man' was one phrase that might have been used.*

Catchphrases that regularly slip into conversation in modern Britain, like 'Oooh, suits you, sir' from television's *The Fast Show* or 'I'm a laydee' from *Little Britain* would mystify anyone who had transported themselves here in a time machine from the 1940s. Similarly, anyone who has not listened to recordings of the radio show *ITMA* (*It's That Man Again*), which ran from 1939 to 1949, would be thoroughly perplexed if Sam and Milner went to leave a room together and paused at the door, saying, 'After you, Cecil,' 'No, after you, Claude.' It means

nothing now but it was a popular catchphrase from *ITMA*, coined by Jack Train and Horace Percival who played Claude and Cecil, the over-polite handymen. Of all the characters in the show, Sam is perhaps the one who is heard to utter the occasional phrase or saying most typical of the 1940s. She uses the term 'tickety-boo' rather than 'okay' and has been known to say goodbye with 'TTFN' (Ta-Ta For Now). Other phrases that would have been used at the time include the words villains used for the police. They were called 'coppers' or 'rozzers', possibly 'bogeys', but never 'filth' or 'pigs'. When it came to romance, people would refer to a courting couple as 'walking out' or 'stepping out,' not 'going out with' or even 'dating'. The words 'boyfriend' and 'girlfriend' were not used at all. 'Her young man' or 'his young lady' was how people referred to the other half of a romantic relationship.

As well as using different phrases, the style of language used by people in everyday situations was also very different to that of today. In *Foyle's War* most people appear to be quite well spoken and, while regional accents were as varied in the 1940s as they are now, the BBC had a massive influence over the way that ordinary people spoke. It was commonly held that BBC announcers spoke English as it was meant to be. Anyone attempting to speak in what they thought to be a 'proper' manner would imitate the voices of the announcers they had heard on the radio and talk 'BBC posh'. The British actors and actresses trained at RADA (Royal Academy of Dramatic Art) that people heard in the cinema or on stage spoke with equal affectation.

Just as they tended to use more formal language, people's general attitude and everyday behaviour were also more formal. 'Foyle would have referred to less senior colleagues by their second names,' says Charman. 'Sergeant Milner would have been "Milner" and other officers "Smith" or "Jones". As a subordinate, Milner would never have expected to be invited into Foyle's home and, on the whole, I think that this is something they get pretty much correct in the series.' Although the rule would have been formality rather than familiarity, perhaps the exception would have been Sam. As we will see later, young ladies such as Sam were often a law unto themselves.

Charman is a great admirer of the series and of the actors who appear in it, but he does have one minor comment about their appearance which, he believes, is an issue no modern drama can ever hope to tackle. 'The attention to detail that goes into the 1940s costumes is impressive,' he says, 'but no one who did not live in the 1940s really knows how to wear those clothes. Milner, for example, looks slightly awkward in a hat. In old movies like *Waterloo Road*, people knew how to wear hats, how to dress in 1940s clothes. You can get the period detail right, but the actors will always look slightly out of place in the old clothes because, for example, gentlemen nowadays do not wear hats like that.

'The other thing that doesn't look quite right is the way today's actors, even though they may actually be a bit older than the characters they are playing, tend to look too young. People in the 1940s, as you can see from old photographs, in old movies and even in old newsreels, looked (to us nowadays at least) much older. This may have been partly due to their diet – they didn't eat as well as we do nowadays – and partly due to smoking. Smoking would certainly have contributed to this prematurely aged look. In the 1940s almost everyone smoked. We see it on screen from time to time in the series, but it is almost inconceivable that neither Milner nor Foyle would be smokers. Offices, bars and anywhere else where a few people gathered together would be cloaked in a haze of cigarette smoke.'

While the costumes are kept as accurate as possible and the dialogue given a 1940s tone, keeping the characters true to life means knowing something of their backgrounds. This means the experiences that have shaped their personalities can be borne in mind when deciding how a character should react in any given situation. The main characters in *Foyle's War* have all lived lives markedly different from one another.

ABOVE: *Christopher Foyle (Michael Kitchen) fought in World War I, having enlisted in the army rather than being conscripted. His undoubted patriotism aside, Foyle almost certainly had his own reasons for joining the army and going to war.*

Christopher Foyle

Detective Chief Superintendent Christopher Foyle carries the authority of his office with the kind of calm confidence that comes with his many years of experience in the police force. He is never heard to raise his voice, a few sharp remarks being all that ever betrays the fact that feelings of anger or frustration are being subdued. Staying in control is one of Foyle's great strengths. He seldom allows anything to distract him from the task at hand and approaches problems in a thoroughly methodical manner, pursuing his enquiries with in meticulous detail. In 'The German Woman' his request for a full autopsy on the murdered Greta Beaumont despite the cause of her death being so obvious (near decapitation on a piano wire strung across the path where she rode her horse) leads to the exposure of her influential husband and those colluding with him to avoid his wife suffering inconvenience under the internment rules. Undoubtedly Foyle's logical mind has been inherited by Andrew, his son, who studied mathematics at Oxford University before volunteering for the RAF.

Having his son flying in the front line during the Battle of Britain causes Foyle a great deal of anguish. His position as a senior police officer makes him acutely aware that Britain, especially his part of the south coast, is in imminent danger of invasion by the Germans. He also knows that pilots like Andrew have very little chance of surviving the war completely unscathed. In 'Eagle Day' the two sit down for a father-son talk, Andrew having asked his father the question that was almost taboo in polite circles, no one ever daring to risk evoking traumatic memories in old soldiers: 'Have you ever killed a man?' Foyle admits that he has done so during

the Great War, advising Andrew that 'you get through it.' In fact, Foyle volunteered for service in World War I, conscription not coming into play until 1916, and went off to war with his friend Fielding, the two of them only a year or so older than Andrew.

There was a great deal of social pressure on young men to enlist when Britain went to war in 1914, something far less in evidence 25 years later. Those who did not sign up and who had no apparent reason for not rushing to enlist could find themselves social outcasts, sneered at by their neighbours in the street or sent white feathers – the mark of a coward – in the post. The war of 1914–18 changed many things, including, to a great extent, this jingoism among the general public. There had never been a war where so many young men had met such inglorious deaths, floundering in the mud of the trenches. Neither had so many died before. Around 750,000 men from Britain were killed, with many more wounded, leading this to be dubbed 'the lost generation'. It was also the first modern war, where machine guns, tanks and aircraft were used to dreadful effect. But the war did not stay in far-off European fields, for German aircraft bombed the British mainland. Although in 1939 the declaration of war was met with an outburst of patriotic fervour perhaps with the prospect of it reaching their own doorsteps, people were a little less inclined to regard warfare as a gallant challenge for the youth of the nation.

Foyle almost certainly had his own, private reason for enlisting. He had met and fallen in love with a girl called Elizabeth, even asking her to marry him. Unfortunately, Elizabeth's father did not approve of the young Foyle, regarding a humble policeman's son as being well below the social standing of an acceptable suitor for his daughter. Elizabeth would not go against her father's wishes, leaving Foyle heartbroken. She later had cause to regret her actions, as we discover in 'Fifty Ships', when the two are reunited. Elizabeth had married a lawyer but had never been happy in the relationship. She had even named her second son Christopher.

Foyle fought in the trenches but survived the war rather better than his friend Fielding who, it was revealed in 'Bad Blood,' was suffering from the after-effects of a gas attack at Yprès. For three years Foyle served in the army, receiving field promotions as he describes it 'by necessity', so many of his superiors having been killed in action. He won the respect and friendship of his commanding officer, the two keeping in touch after their return from France, with Foyle becoming godfather to his former CO's daughter, Lydia. Discharged with the rank of an 'acting officer', he exchanged one uniform for another almost immediately by following in his father's footsteps and joining the police force.

Before long he met another young woman, Rosalind. She was to become the love of his life. They married and together had Andrew but when their son was only 10 or 11 years old, Rosalind contracted typhoid and died. Typhoid is a bacterial infection transmitted through contaminated food or drinking water and causes a very unpleasant fever. It is relatively rare in Britain today, modern hygiene standards keeping it at bay, although cases do still crop up, most sufferers having contracted the disease abroad. Queen Victoria's husband, Prince Albert, famously died of the condition in 1861 but even in the 1930s typhoid remained a very serious illness, difficult to treat without today's range of antibiotics. A

major outbreak in Croydon in 1937 claimed a total of 43 lives.

So Foyle was left to bring up Andrew on his own while pursuing his career in the police force. That he rose through the ranks to become a Detective Chief Superintendent demonstrates his dedication to his profession, but his highly-developed sense of fair play and determination to uphold the law often resulted in conflict. One sergeant who worked with him, Jack Devlin, earned his contempt when he 'manufactured' evidence in a case. Devlin was to return as an army officer in the episode entitled 'War Games'.

Foyle clashed with his superiors, too. His repeated requests to be transferred out of Hastings to a position – perhaps in military intelligence – where his military experience, his command of the German language and the skills acquired in the police force might be better used to help the war effort cause a great deal of friction. But why should he be left in Hastings? A number of prominent police officers had, after all, transferred to other duties. Chief Inspector Campion of Scotland Yard had become Major Campion, in charge of the Military Police Special Investigation Branch. Commander Leonard Burt was transferred to MI5. After the war he was to escort 'Lord Haw-Haw', otherwise known as William Joyce, from Germany to Britain to face trial for treason. Foyle is utterly frustrated by the fact that his superiors had obviously decided there was to be no such role for him.

But it is the fact that the law can be bent or broken by those in authority in the belief that the war changes all of the rules of law and order – the values by which Foyle sets so much store – that leads Foyle eventually to consider his own usefulness as a police officer, and whether he should continue in the role.

ABOVE: *In 'Fifty Ships' Foyle was reunited with Elizabeth (Amanda Root), the love of his life prior to his military service and his marriage to Rosalind, who died of typhoid.*

ABOVE: *Detective Sergeant Paul Milner (Anthony Howell) was in the Territorial Army and lost the lower part of his left leg while fighting in Norway in 1940.*

Paul Milner

Detective Sergeant Paul Milner is a very lucky man. In working with DCS Foyle he has landed the job he always wanted, ever since he was a child. As a schoolboy his hero was Bulldog Drummond, the former army officer from World War I who set up his own private detective agency to root out villainy of all sorts in England during the 1920s and 1930s. Young Milner snooped around neighbours' properties whenever he suspected that an evil anarchist or despicable Trotskyite might be hatching a plot to place the country in peril. In the end, the peril Milner was to see Britain confront came not from an enemy within, but from the rise of Nazism in Germany. The ensuing conflict was to demonstrate that Milner was, indeed, a very lucky man.

In joining the police service when he left school, Milner aimed to fulfil his ambition of becoming a detective. He was doing rather well at it, too, having earned himself a good enough reputation for Foyle to ask him to become his sergeant. On that occasion, he turned Foyle down. He spent some time stationed in Catford and in Brighton and, as his career developed, so too did his personal life. He married Jane, whom he had known since they were at school together, and began to enjoy a settled, comfortable existence. When war broke out, however, there was no keeping him at home. Well, Bulldog Drummond wouldn't have stayed behind, would he?

Milner was a member of the Territorial Army, Britain's part-time volunteer reserve force, and soon found himself full-time in khaki uniform, training for action in Norway. Once the Germans had overrun Poland in 1939 and the Allies declared war there was a momentary lull in hostilities as the opposing sides braced themselves for war in mainland Europe. The Germans, in fact, were casting

their eyes north to the neutral states of Denmark and Norway. Denmark was of little real strategic importance to Germany, but Norway was far more valuable for two main reasons. As a base for naval operations it allowed U-boats and the surface fleet access to the North Atlantic, where they could prey on Allied convoys. Also, Germany's main supply of iron ore, vital to her industrial output, came from Sweden via the Norwegian port of Narvik. On 9 April 1940 the Germans invaded Denmark and Norway, taking Denmark with little resistance. The same was not true of Norway. The Norwegian armed forces fought ferociously to defend their country, but within 24 hours the Germans had taken their major objectives, including Narvik. Off the Norwegian coast the British Royal Navy engaged elements of the German Kriegsmarine in deadly duels. Two naval battles were fought off Narvik alone, with the Germans losing no less than eight destroyers in the second battle.

On 16 April the first elements of an Allied force comprising British, French and Polish troops landed in Norway intent on retaking Narvik. The next day further landings took place near Trondheim with the aim of taking the German garrison there and linking up with Norwegian units still in the field. It was as part of this group that Corporal Paul Milner would have fought. Lacking adequate air support, the untried Allied troops faced up to battle-hardened German veterans while being bombarded from the sky and shelled from the fjords by German warships sheltering there. After ten days it became clear that Allied troops must be pulled out of the Trondheim area if they were not all to be lost. They were evacuated by 3 May, having suffered appalling casualties. Within a week the Germans launched their offensive against Holland, Belgium, Luxembourg and France, and by the end of the first week in

June, Allied troops had been evacuated from France and Norway.

Milner was one of the many thousands of casualties from the ill-fated Norwegian campaign. He lost his left leg below the knee, and would have lost his life had it not been for his friend, Will Grayson, who dragged him to safety. In 'Invasion' Will appears in Hastings on leave only to lose his life in a house fire having blinded himself drinking illicit hooch.

Victims of accidents, or those like Milner who have been wounded in battle, testify to the fact that losing a limb is a traumatic experience not only with regard to the physical wound but also in terms of its psychological impact. The effect has been likened to grieving for a close relative in that something integral to your life has suddenly been taken away. Milner suffered a great deal of mental anguish as a result of his experiences in Norway and this, as well as her inability to cope with the fact that he had lost a leg, was what his wife blamed for having driven her to leave him. She claimed he was no longer the same person and departed for Wales to live with her sister. Jane reappears briefly only to walk in on Milner and Sam enjoying a meal together when he offers Sam the spare room after her house is bombed in 'Fifty Ships'. After that, he wasn't to see her again for over two years.

While it is not strictly true to say that they were divorced, Milner intimated to Foyle some time after Jane's departure that this was the case. He also allows an old flame, Edith Ashford, to believe he is divorced when she turns up at the station asking for help on her brother's behalf in 'Bad Blood'. It is most unlike the scrupulously honest Milner to perpetrate such a deceit, but the subterfuge is understandable given the circumstances and the fact that, as one who likes to be in control of his life, this loose end is hugely

frustrating to him. At that time the divorce laws were such that the Milners' marriage would have been over if he could accuse Jane of 'desertion'. For that, she would have to stay away for at least three years. But she didn't. Just as Milner feels that love is blossoming with Edith, Jane returns, claiming she wants to move home and try to make their marriage work again. Even if Milner had been willing to try to rekindle their relationship, it was too late for Jane: an old friend involved her in dark dealings with a desperate criminal, who ultimately murdered them both.

Unfortunately, given that the circumstances of his marriage are now known, Milner becomes the prime suspect for the murder of his wife. Only Foyle's belief in his innocence and dogged pursuit of the truth saves him from the gallows.

Samantha Stewart

Foyle and Milner are the sort of detective double act you might expect to find in a murder mystery series, but Sam is something of a cuckoo in the nest. A Detective Chief Superintendent would certainly have had a driver, but it would have been more likely to be a police sergeant than an MTC (Mechanised Transport Corps) volunteer. The police even had the Women's Auxiliary Police Corps female drivers to chauffeur senior officers, but not every force in the country employed women. Although unusual, it is not beyond the realms of possibility that wartime staff shortages and the fact that Sam knows the roads around the south coast might just have left a detective like Foyle with a driver like Sam. Ironically, while Sam is something of an 'odd one out', she is also the only one of the characters devised by Anthony Horowitz who is actually based on a real person.

When he was a little boy, Anthony had a nanny (perhaps more properly termed a governess) called Norah Fitzgerald, who was a WAAF driver during World War II. He could listen to Norah's tales of her wartime adventures for hours. Grown-ups are constantly telling young children that they need to behave themselves and that they shouldn't be naughty, so it is always hugely entertaining for them to hear stories about grown-ups misbehaving in the most outrageous manner. Norah didn't disappoint. Her stories were generally about sneaking back into her quarters late at night, long after she was supposed to have been tucked up in bed, having been out drinking and dancing in places she was not supposed to frequent. Known to her superior officers and friends as 'Fitzy,' she told Anthony about her marvellous life in uniform and all the fun she had driving important people in a motor car at a time when most girls like her were not expected to be going out to work at all. There was also, however, almost inevitably, a sad side to her stories: she fell in love with a pilot and was devastated when he was killed during the Battle of Britain. Sam, then, is Anthony's tribute to Fitzy, a feisty, intelligent, inquisitive young woman who relishes the prospect of making her mark in an unfamiliar world.

ABOVE: *Vicar's daughter Samantha Stewart (Honeysuckle Weeks) caused a stir, not least with Foyle, when she was appointed as his personal driver.*

ABOVE: *It would have been unusual for a senior police officer like Foyle to have had a driver who was not at least a police sergeant and quite extraordinary, although not impossible, for an MTC driver like Sam to have been given the job.*

She was born and brought up in Lyminster, just outside Arundel in West Sussex. Her father was the vicar of St Stephen's Church, and in 'Eagle Day' we learn that her mother is not in good health. Her father, Iain, turns up in Hastings to demand that Sam should give up her job as Foyle's driver, cast aside the wanton lifestyle of a woman in uniform and return home where she belongs. Only Foyle's understated powers of persuasion bring the Reverend Stewart to realise that Sam is a vital part of his team, and she remains as Foyle's driver.

To his great annoyance, Sam begins her work with Foyle as an inquisitive, enthusiastic and talkative young woman who believes the war has given her an unmissable opportunity to get away from her suffocating life at the vicarage in Lyminster. Volunteering to join the MTC was her escape route. The MTC taught women to be mechanics and drivers, and a girl with Sam's background would have been seen as ideal for driving high-ranking military personnel from place to place.

Women like Sam were most likely to already have some driving experience. At that time most people did not own cars and anyone from a working-class family, male or female, would be unlikely ever to have learned to drive unless they had been taught in the armed forces or as part of their job – bus drivers, truck drivers or taxi drivers. It was also felt by some that young ladies from a middle-class background would be better suited to discipline and the military life. A young woman who knew how to drive and, like Sam, had some mechanical aptitude would have been snapped up. Sam, as we discover in 'They Fought In The Fields,' has a farmer cousin who let her mess around with his tractors.

Diana Pitt Parsons studied art prior to becoming a WAAF and training as a radar operator in 1940. As she explains, 'A lot of the girls in radar had been to boarding schools – they chose those girls of that background. And I always insist that, after a girls' boarding school anything would be quite blissful. Being in the WAAF was freedom after knowing what a girls' school could be like.'[1]

Sam, then, is not untypical of the type of girl to be found driving for officers in the early years of the war. Driving for an army officer should not have been too risky an occupation. During her adventures with Foyle, on the other hand, she is bombed, shot at, assaulted, works undercover, finds romance, declines a proposal of marriage and contracts anthrax. Those sorts of things don't ordinarily happen to a vicar's daughter. Although at first extremely unsure of her Foyle soon comes to realise the value of having a young woman with a fresh approach and a lively mind on his team. Sam's romance with his son, Andrew, was initially kept from him but he comes to accept it, just as he has to deal with the awkwardness between him

and Sam when Andrew, posted to a training squadron miles away, ends the relationship in a letter to Sam.

In the episode 'Bad Blood,' when Sam is lying in hospital having been infected with anthrax, Foyle's concern and genuine affection for her shine through. Any last lingering doubts that Sam may have had about being a real part of Foyle's team evaporate into thin air.

ABOVE: *Unlike most of the other characters in* Foyle's War, *Sam is partly based on a real person, writer Anthony Horowitz having used his childhood governess as his inspiration for the character.*

[1] *WWII: The People's Story*, Michael O'Mara Books for Reader's Digest 2003

ABOVE: *Andrew Foyle (Julian Ovenden) abandoned his mathematics degree at Oxford University to train as a Spitfire pilot.*

Andrew Foyle

Andrew Foyle's relationship with his father has outgrown the awkwardness of his teenage years and moved on to a far more adult footing. The two are able to chat while sharing some of Foyle's favourite Glenlivet malt whisky and even go fishing together, although Foyle is well aware that Andrew does so out of duty rather than sharing his love of the sport. However, they are not on such equal terms that Andrew can feel entirely comfortable about informing his father of decisions he has made that he is well aware will meet with Foyle's disapproval. Abandoning his mathematics degree at Oxford to train as a fighter pilot with the RAF is one of those decisions. He would certainly not have been alone.

In September 1939 the RAF's Volunteer Reserve, based at small airstrips and university flying clubs all over the country, numbered around 60,000. The aircraft on which they trained were largely outdated. Not all of the university fliers were to make fighter pilots, but they were among the first to be called up. The young men who flew in the Battle of Britain fascinate Anthony Horowitz and he is full of admiration for them. Although Foyle is not based on any one individual, Anthony did draw on the experiences of two very famous pilots, Richard Hillary and Geoffrey Wellum, when developing the character of his son. When war broke out Richard Hillary was a student at Oxford, Secretary of the University Boat Club and President of the Rugby Club. Hillary had also joined the Volunteer Reserve in 1938. He was called up less than a month after war was declared. Hillary described the elation at first flying a Spitfire in his book, *The Last Enemy*, which was published as a propaganda exercise during the war but has since gained much critical acclaim.

Kilmartin swung himself on to a wing and started to run through the instruments. I was conscious of his voice, but heard nothing of what he said. I was to fly a Spitfire. It was what I had most wanted through all the long dreary months of training. If I could fly a Spitfire, it would be worth it.

Once in the air, Hillary demonstrated to himself why flying such a machine was a young man's game. He was just 21 at the time.

I wanted ample room for mistakes and possible blacking-out. With one or two very sharp movements on the stick I blacked myself out for a few seconds, but the machine was sweeter to handle than any other that I had flown.

Blacking out was caused by the G-forces of high-speed turns which drained the blood from the pilots' brains, causing them to lose consciousness for a few moments. Young, fit men would quickly regain consciousness and immediately re-orientate themselves. Older pilots could take a lot longer – long enough to mean the difference between regaining control of the aircraft or plummeting to earth; long enough for an enemy pilot to latch onto you. In the late summer of 1940 Hillary was with 603 Squadron based at Hornchurch in Essex, in the thick of the Battle of Britain. He shot down five enemy aircraft and was downed twice, the second time suffering horrendous burns to his hands and face.

Andrew Foyle, of course, is not immediately posted to an operational squadron on completing his training.

He is instead given a secret assignment on the south coast, testing the effectiveness of the radar installations by flying his Spitfire low and fast to try to evade detection. It is not long, however, before he is in the thick of it and, once he has done his bit and seems on the verge of succumbing to stress, the experiences of the second real-life pilot on which Anthony Horowitz drew are brought into play. Geoffrey Wellum is the author of *First Light*, an account of his experiences in the Battle of Britain and beyond, vividly recalled despite the fact that it was written 35 years later. He survived the dog-fights and subsequent wartime service to become an RAF instructor. That, of course, is also what happens to Andrew.

RIGHT: *The pilots who fought in the Battle of Britain flew the most technologically advanced aircraft in the world, yet they were all in their late teens or early twenties. Only the youngest and fittest were able to cope with the rigours of flying a fighter plane in combat.*

4. Truth & Fiction

Each episode of *Foyle's War* has a number of different historical wartime
themes woven into the plot and each of these themes has its basis in fact,
as do many of the crimes that Foyle becomes involved in investigating. The
turmoil through which people lived during the war years threw up all sorts
of bizarre situations, making the facts behind some of the Foyle's war
storylines even stranger than the fiction.

The German Woman

In this first episode of *Foyle's War*, Detective Chief Superintendent
Christopher Foyle finds his latest efforts to secure a transfer out of
Hastings into a job where he might feel he was doing more to help the war
effort thwarted yet again by his superior, Assistant Commissioner Summers.
Instead of a transfer, he is promised a driver. The driver (who Foyle has
been told is called Stewart) duly reports for duty and, to his surprise, turns
out to be a volunteer in army uniform from the Mechanised Transport
Corps (MTA). Even more surprising is the fact that Sam Stewart is a young
woman – Samantha.

ABOVE: *Although* Foyle's War *is always as historically accurate as possible, there are occasions, such as the remarkably swift recovery of Paul Milner from his traumatic operation, where the truth has to be stretched slightly.*

It would certainly have been most unusual, as Foyle himself says, for 'a ranking officer' to be assigned a driver from outside of the police service. At that time, however, personnel shortages might have made Sam's involvement possible. The third member of Foyle's team, Detective Sergeant Milner, is still in hospital recovering from a serious wound sustained while fighting in the ill-fated Norwegian campaign as Foyle begins investigating the murder of Greta Beaumont, the German-born wife of a local magistrate. Nevertheless, Foyle enlists the help of the thoroughly dispirited Milner and he and Sam are even there to meet him when he hobbles out of the hospital on crutches at the end of the story. This was a much faster recovery rate than anyone in Milner's situation could ever have had in real life. Milner had lost a leg and recuperating after such a traumatic wound normally took months. Learning to walk with a prosthetic limb was another long and painful experience for those unfortunate enough to have to do so. *Foyle's War*, however, as we should always remember, is fiction created primarily for entertainment and, while every effort is made to maintain historical accuracy, certain allowances have to be made to keep the storylines running smoothly.

The murder of the fictional Greta Beaumont is set at a time when feelings among the general population were running particularly high against foreigners, especially Germans, on British soil. Prior to the Nazi party coming to power in Germany there were around 20,000 German nationals living in Britain. This number swelled dramatically as the flood of mainly Jewish refugees poured out of Germany, Austria and Czechoslovakia. At the outbreak of the war there were over 70,000 Germans and Austrians who could be considered 'enemy aliens'. While the popular press called for all such foreigners to be interned, the authorities simply had

ABOVE: *The disdain shown by many towards German-born Greta Beaumont (Joanna Kanska) reflected the way that 'enemy aliens' were treated by former friends and neighbours.*

nowhere to put them. Disused cotton mills were pressed into service as squalid 'prisons', camps of tents established, Billy Smart's Circus's winter camp at Ascot racecourse in Surrey became a detention camp while many internees found themselves incarcerated in purpose-built prisons on the Isle of Man. One option was to ship internees abroad to Canada, although this practice came to an end when a German submarine torpedoed

ABOVE: *Anyone branded an 'enemy alien' who was thought to pose a security risk could find themselves incarcerated in makeshift prisons that included disused cotton mills and a camp of tents in the middle of Ascot racecourse.*

and sank the *Arandora Star*, 800 on board losing their lives.

Once registered, the 'enemy aliens' were assessed according to the security risk they posed and classified accordingly. Aliens classified 'A' were interned. Those given a 'B' classification were restricted in how far from home they were allowed to travel and 'C' class aliens were allowed to go free. The regulations were later tightened up, with those B-class aliens living in coastal areas rounded up and imprisoned. C-class aliens had curfews imposed upon them and, in fact, by the summer of 1940 most B- and C-class aliens had been locked up. Those left at large were not allowed to own cars, maps or even bicycles.

Many of the refugees classed as enemy aliens had fled from the prospect of being imprisoned in camps by the Germans in Europe. To be interned in Britain caused them great distress, especially as families were split asunder, men separated from their wives. On the Isle of Wight the men were kept at Peveril Camp in Peel while the women were sent to Rusden Camp in Port Erin several miles away. The situation deteriorated even further when Italy declared war on the Allies in June 1940. Four thousand Italians, who had lived in Britain for less than 20 years, were immediately interned.

Many Italians were, perhaps, in an even worse position than the Germans. The businesses they tended to run were restaurants or ice-cream parlours, often in coastal resorts from which enemy aliens of any classification were banned. Italian shops all over the country were attacked by mobs, their windows smashed and stock strewn across the streets. Police in Cardiff, among other places, found themselves in the peculiar position of having to mount baton charges to disperse rioting crowds bent on destroying Italian-owned businesses when they had previously visited such premises to arrest the owners as potential enemies of the state. In 'A Lesson In Murder', Foyle's favourite Italian restaurant, Carlo's, was destroyed when a mob threw a Molotov cocktail through the window, killing Foyle's old friend Carlo.

The process of being arrested as an enemy alien was traumatic, degrading and humiliating. Police officers would arrive out of the blue and take individuals or entire families into custody. Needless to say, this was not done without attracting the attention of inquisitive locals and crowds were quick to gather. Internees could then find themselves taunted with racial abuse, or have former neighbours sneering at them and calling them spies as they were marched into the street. In other cases, friends and neighbours were outraged, knowing full well that some of those being placed under arrest, especially the Italians, had fought alongside the British in World War I, or had sons who had been called up to serve with the British armed forces. Tribunals were established to review the cases of those interned and many were released within a short while. By 1943 around 90 per cent of all enemy aliens were released to take up jobs, where they contributed to the war effort or even for service with the British military.

In *Foyle's War* the German woman, of course, was not murdered simply because she was German but because she had become entangled in a far darker web of passion, jealousy, greed and deceit – all motives that could have brought about her demise, whether or not there was a war raging.

The White Feather

The evacuation of Allied troops from the beaches at Dunkirk formed the backdrop to 'The White Feather' with local fishermen setting off to join the fleet of more than 860 vessels of all shapes and sizes that played a part in rescuing the besieged soldiers. A real Hastings fishing boat belonging to local fisherman Graham Bossom was used as the *Lady Rose* when 'The White Feather' was filmed. Back in 1940, although ten fishing boats from Hastings answered the call for help, heading to Dover to offer their services on 30 May, none of them actually crossed the channel to participate in the evacuation. On the other hand, the Hastings lifeboat, *The Cyril and Lilian Bishop*, was taken to France to help pluck men from the beaches. She was crewed by Royal Navy personnel and returned to Hastings after the event, battered and bruised, but having done her duty. The lifeboat may have been deemed more suitable than the fishing boats because, despite the Hastings boats being beach-launched whenever they put to sea, they launched from the beach empty, carrying little or no weight. There was a danger with some boats that they could, when overloaded with weary, waterlogged soldiers, stick fast in the sand and become sitting ducks.

One fleet of fishing boats seen as ideal for working close in to the Dunkirk beaches was the Leigh-on-Sea cockle boats. Used to working the unpredictable shallow waters of the Thames estuary off the Essex shore, the idea was that the Leigh fishermen would take their boats as near to the French beaches as they could, the boats' shallow draft of just two feet allowing them to pluck men

ABOVE: *In 'The White Feather', a Hastings fisherman (Ian Hogg) takes his boat and his son to help the rescue effort at Dunkirk. The Hastings fishing boats were offered but not required for Dunkirk, although the Hastings lifeboat did make the trip.*

from the water far closer to shore than most other craft. Some crews even tied up at the jetty off Dunkirk to go ashore and persuade reluctant soldiers that their little 36-foot long boats were perfectly seaworthy. Six boats from Leigh made the trip – *Defender, Letitia, Resolute, Endeavour, Reliance* and *Renown*. In eight gruelling hours they ferried 1,200 troops out to the larger ships waiting offshore. *Letitia*'s rudder was damaged and she was taken in tow for the journey home on 1 June, and *Renown* broke down to be taken in tow behind *Letitia*. Shortly afterwards, *Renown* struck a mine. Her crew, Leigh cousins Frank Osborne, Leslie Osborne and Harry Noakes, were lost along with Harold Porter, a naval rating from Birmingham assigned to the boat.

The entire episode of 'The White Feather' was not, of course, devoted solely to the drama unfolding across the channel. It began with Foyle interviewing a young woman arrested for sabotage, having cut some phone lines. She was convinced the Germans would be storming the beaches of England's south coast and marching through the streets of Hastings within days. In real life there were many like her. A woman on the Isle of Wight was sentenced to death for cutting military phone lines, although her sentence was later reduced to 14 years' penal servitude. Some believed that if they were found in jail for committing such acts when the Germans came, the invaders would treat them less harshly. For others, sabotage – especially in

ABOVE: *Around 860 vessels of all sizes were involved in bringing home over 330,000 allied soldiers from Dunkirk in a desperate evacuation from the beaches between 28 May and 3 June 1940.*

the workplace – was more a matter of petty vindictiveness, a way of settling a score for having missed out on a promotion or a pay rise. Naturally, there were also politically motivated saboteurs. Communists working in the shipyards caused damage to vessels as a way of protesting against the war. There were pacifists like the Manchester man who sabotaged components used on vehicles for the Ministry of Supply in May 1941 because he felt the war was fundamentally wrong and that he had to try to stop it in any way he could. The most disturbing and sinister political force in the country, however, was the Fascist movement.

Sergeant Milner flirted briefly with the idea of joining an ultra-right wing organisation in 'The White Feather' when he attended a meeting held by the debonair Guy Spencer. A leading member of a group called The Friday Club, Spencer had pro-Hitler, anti-Semitic views which Milner found abhorrent, although he did fall under Spencer's charismatic spell for a while. His interest in Spencer had, perhaps, been roused by patriotism and an understandable

disappointment at the way he felt he and his fellow soldiers had been let down in Norway. But it didn't take him long to realise that Spencer and his followers were inspired by hatred rather than an honourable national loyalty. Both Foyle and Milner were forced to take further interest in Spencer's group when Margaret Ellis, the owner of The White Feather Hotel, who played host to Spencer and his cronies, was shot dead.

A number of Fascist or extreme right-wing groups existed in Britain at the beginning of the war and several prominent society figures were interned because of their activities with such groups. Midlothian and Peebles MP Captain Archibald Ramsay founded The Right Club, which espoused anti-Semitic views. He was locked up in Brixton Prison, along with Admiral Sir Barry Domville, a leading light in The Link, an organisation that promoted friendship and co-operation with Germany. The most famous British Fascist, of course, was Sir Oswald Moseley, who had attended the Royal Military Academy, Sandhurst and fought with the 16th Lancers during World War I

RIGHT: *Sergeant Milner was intrigued by the philosophies of a right-wing group called The Friday Club. Their anti-Semitic stance was common to a number of real-life organisations in the 1930s and 1940s.*

ABOVE: *Guy Spencer (Charles Dance) claimed to be a patriot but had dubious motives, wanted Britain to take no part in the war against Germany and was prepared to collaborate with the enemy to achieve his goals.*

before transferring to the Royal Flying Corps and sustaining injuries in a plane crash that ended his war in 1916. He became the youngest Member of Parliament when he won Harrow for the Conservatives in 1918, retaining the seat as an independent in 1922 and crossing the house to join the Labour party in 1924. Rising through the ranks, he was appointed Chancellor of the Duchy of Lancaster when Ramsay Macdonald became Prime Minister in 1930.

Moseley grew disillusioned with Labour politics, however, and resigned, forming his own New Party in 1931, only to disband

ABOVE: *Sir Oswald Moseley, leader of the British Union of Fascists, was imprisoned along with his wife in Brixton Prison where they lived together in an apartment rather than normal jail cells.*

it within a year or so after a visit to Italy. Mussolini's style of leadership apparently impressed him so much that he formed the British Union of Fascists. The anti-Semitic views expressed by the BUF, whose numbers had swelled to around 30,000 by 1934, led to violent clashes when the brown-shirted marchers attempted to parade through predominantly Jewish areas of London's East End. When Moseley was interned, he and his wife were permitted special privileges, living together in an apartment within Brixton Prison. The BUF was disbanded, banned from producing any kind of publication and its organisers were imprisoned.

But there were other right-wing groups active in the political arena that had far greater influence in the corridors of power than Moseley's brown-shirts could ever have hoped to achieve. Communist journalist Claud Cockburn coined the phrase 'The Cliveden Set' to describe the group which met at Cliveden, the home of Lord and Lady Astor. The term was soon taken up by the popular press. Among the set were the Astors, Lord Lothian and Lord Halifax, as well as a number of other aristocrats and wealthy industrialists. Lord Halifax became Secretary for War in 1935 and Foreign Secretary under Prime Minister Neville Chamberlain in 1938, and one of the members of The Friday Club in 'The White Feather' is described as working in Lord Halifax's office. Chamberlain also had close connections with the set, regularly visiting Cliveden. The group was almost certainly able to cajole, persuade and otherwise influence British Government policy. Far from being traitors, they saw themselves as a kind of think tank, using all of their influence to promote peace in Europe by appeasing the Nazis. They believed a strong German state would act as a buffer between Western Europe and the Communists in the East. They were prepared to overlook, if not

openly condone the behaviour of the Nazis towards the Jews and other minority races. Even after the government issued a White Paper in October 1939 detailing some of the horrors of camps such as Buchenwald, they pressed for the British Government to come to a settlement with Germany. Lord Halifax was still arguing for a peace when Churchill took over from Chamberlain and the British Army was forced into the sea at Dunkirk. Churchill retained him as Foreign Secretary long enough for the government to show a united front against the Germans but by the end of 1940 he was replaced as Foreign Secretary, becoming Britain's ambassador to the United States instead.

Foyle ensures his clash with the leader of The Friday Club, Guy Spencer, ends with Spencer heading for prison, having tried to send a sensitive document to the Germans. Naturally, while working out exactly what Spencer was up to, he also manages to identify the murderer of Margaret Ellis.

A Lesson In Murder
When a prisoner is found hanged in a police cell in Hastings in the episode 'A Lesson In Murder', Foyle suspects all is not quite as it seems. Threats are then issued against a local magistrate and Foyle is sent to investigate, quickly coming to suspect that the two incidents may be connected. At the magistrate's expansive country house a small boy, evacuated from London to live with the family, is then killed in an explosion and the magistrate himself subsequently shot dead. The dead prisoner and the magistrate were known to each other because the magistrate presided over the tribunal at which the prisoner presented his claims to be a Conscientious Objector. Quite how the suicide, the murder and the death of the young boy are tied together is an intrigue that becomes ever more tragic as Foyle's

enquiries draw him towards the truth. The vital clue comes from the notebook of the dead evacuee.

The little boy who met such a sad end in 'A Lesson In Murder' was not entirely typical of the children evacuated from Britain's cities during the war. Wherever possible, children were sent into the countryside as families, brothers and sisters being billeted together. For most of them it was a horrendous wrench, being separated from their mothers for the first time and, for children who had been brought up, for example, in London's East End, seeing open countryside for the first time in their lives was a revelation. Used to bricks and concrete at every turn, the rolling fields of Somerset or Wiltshire were like a different world. Not every child had to leave their mother behind, though. Where a baby or infant was involved, the mother was evacuated as well, meaning some families were evacuated with brothers, sisters and mum all together. For others, school was their link with home. Whole schools were evacuated to the same location, accompanied by the teachers, and the evacuees went to school in village halls or meeting rooms with all their old classmates. This helped to foster animosity between local children and the 'outsiders', leading to bullying and victimisation. Even when the youngsters arrived they weren't always welcomed with open arms. Parading through the streets of High Wycombe, having been evacuated by train from London, four-year-old Sylvia Townson remembers locals gathering on the streets to watch them walk from the station. She was with her mother, who later told her that the crowds were shouting abuse, calling them refugees.

The misery of evacuation led to some children running away, heading for home. For others the whole experience was a great adventure and they kept in touch with their adoptive parents for years after the war. Around 1.5 million children and mothers were evacuated from the cities in 1939 but by early 1940, the 'phoney war' having seen no real dangers visited upon their homes, more than half had drifted back to town. This prompted a second wave of evacuations when the bombs started to fall. Seaside towns, with their abundant holiday accommodation, were seen as ideal destinations for evacuees. In the north, children from cities like Hull were evacuated to Scarborough, with hotel bedrooms turned into school dormitories. In the south Hastings was one of the seaside towns that played host to an influx of youngsters. Around 3,000 arrived at the beginning of September 1939, as well as

BELOW: *Joe Cooper (Gregg Prentice) was an evacuee sent out of London to the safety of the countryside.*

ABOVE: *Joe was billeted with magistrate Lawrence Gascoigne (Oliver Ford Davies), his wife Emily (Cheryl Campbell) and daughter Susan (Sophia Myles).*

hundreds of patients from London hospitals, who were found beds in the three main hospitals around the town. Nine months after their arrival, when Hastings looked to be standing in the front line of a German invasion, the children were re-evacuated, some sent as far afield as Wales. They were shortly to be followed by the children of Hastings, who were evacuated, school by school, to towns in Hertfordshire and Bedfordshire.

The war meant that children were shunted from pillar to post all over the country, but for their fathers and older brothers it meant being called up for military service. In September 1939 the army's strength stood at around 400,000, with about the same number in the part-time Territorial regiments. Clearly, to face up the might of the Wehrmacht many more soldiers would be needed. From May 1939 young men aged 20 to 21 had been required to undertake six months' military training, but as soon as war was declared Parliament passed the National Service (Armed Forces) Act. This provided for conscription of all men between the ages of 18 and 41.

Registration for military service began with men aged between 21 and 23, although within a year this had been extended to 27-year-olds. When they registered, conscripts could opt to serve either with the Army, Navy or RAF. Skilled workers too young to qualify for exemption on the 'reserved occupation' list could find their talents as engineers, mechanics or craftsmen being put to good use in the armed forces, although employers were able to request 'deferment' of military service for workers considered vital to their businesses. Those deemed unfit for military service were obviously exempted, although medical examinations for the military were often less than thorough. One Glasgow conscript was graded A1, fit for service, despite suffering

from St Vitus' Dance, a disorder of the central nervous system causing involuntary muscle spasms in the face and limbs. Since 1931 he had been under the care of a doctor. He was probably suspected of trying to avoid military service as he had also declared himself a Conscientious Objector.

Conscientious Objectors (or COs) were those who objected to being drafted into the services on moral, religious or political grounds. When conscription was introduced during World War I, those who objected were treated most harshly, not only by the authorities but also the general public. During the 1914–18 war there was great pressure on young men to 'do their bit' for king and country. Those who refused were branded cowards, ostracised within their own communities, or sent to prison. The enduring memories of the horrors of the first war may have softened attitudes towards COs by 1939 and, officially at least, the authorities were obliged to adopt a more understanding attitude. The Prime Minister, Neville Chamberlain, stated that those whose beliefs genuinely rendered military service untenable 'should be respected and that there should be no persecution.' In reality, that wasn't always quite how it worked.

Those who declared themselves COs had to go before a tribunal to put their case for exemption. During World War I young men standing before such a tribunal were often subjected to a barrage of abuse in crude attempts to shame them into withdrawing their attempt to register as a CO. In World War II, however, this was not supposed to happen. The panel was generally composed of local figures: there would be a priest or vicar, one of the five-man panel would be appointed with the blessing of the trades unions and a magistrate would chair the hearing. More often than not, however, the panel would

ABOVE: *Around 1.5 million children and mothers were evacuated from Britain's cities in 1939 but by early 1940 over half had drifted back home.*

LEFT: *Judge Gascoigne became hoodlum Jack Winters' (Christopher Fox) sworn enemy when he sentenced Winters to be birched (a type of flogging) and sent to borstal.*

be loaded with old soldiers who had served in the first war and neither understood nor cared to accept the arguments of the would-be COs. They pointed out that, with the entire country at war, almost anything a non-combatant did – saving money in the bank, helping a wounded civilian, fighting a fire in a neighbour's house – would be contributing to the war effort. Almost 60,000 people (women registered as COs after the industrial call-up to industry was announced in December 1941) applied to be exempted from service. Only around 3,500 were granted full exemption, usually on the grounds of their religious beliefs. More than half of the rest were given CO status provided they stayed in their jobs if their work was deemed valuable to the war effort. Or they agreed to take a job on a farm, as a forester or in any number of areas where they could make a valid contribution. Nearly 15,000 ended up in the armed forces, where they were assigned to non-combatant roles, the army setting up a special Non Combatant Corps that eventually grew to be 7,000 strong. There were even CO medics and stretcher-bearers among the first to parachute into France on D-Day in 1944.

Conscientious Objectors were not cowards. A third of the 12,000 whose claims for CO status were totally rejected ended up in the army, where they continued to refuse to undertake military duties and were court-martialled. They then had to face up to the brutal regimes of military prisons, where COs were treated appallingly badly, making the abuse that led to the suicide of the CO in the police cell in 'A Lesson In Murder' all the more horrifyingly authentic.

Eagle Day

Andrew Foyle completes his pilot training with the RAF in 'Eagle Day' and returns home to Hastings, where he is assigned to special duties rather than being sent directly to an operational squadron like most of those with whom he has trained. His special mission is to undertake low-flying exercises, performing mock attacks on the British coast to test the effectiveness of the new radar system. The tests are so top secret that he can't even tell his father what he is doing, although he is able to express his concern about the circumstances surrounding the death of a WAAF who works at the radar research station. Meanwhile, DCS Foyle is

ABOVE: *Special flying operations to test the RAF's new radar systems, like the ones undertaken by Andrew Foyle, did actually happen prior to the Battle of Britain.*

investigating the murder of a man whose
body has been found in a bombed-out
building and discovers links to the theft of
art treasures being shipped to Wales for
safekeeping. He is distracted when Andrew
is arrested for treason, but a connection
between the dead WAAF and the body-in-
The-Blitz helps him prove that Andrew has
been framed.

Radar tests just like the ones in which
Andrew Foyle becomes involved were actually
carried out during World War II. The highly
secret RDF (Radio Direction Finding)
system had been under development for
five years by the time Britain went to war.
Exercises were conducted in 1934 to evaluate
how Britain's defences would stand up to a
bomber offensive and it was found that the
majority of bombers would get through to
their targets unscathed. The Air Ministry
decided to look at developing a 'death ray'
high-power radio beam that could kill pilots
of incoming aircraft. They consulted Scots
scientist Robert Watson-Watt, a descendant
of James Watt (who had developed the steam
engine). Watson-Watt was head of a radio
research laboratory and advised that a death
ray was not feasible but that using radio waves
to detect aircraft was a distinct possibility.

In February 1935 Watson-Watt and his
team successfully used a BBC transmitter
in an exercise to locate an airborne RAF
bomber. Within three months his team
was established at Orfordness in Suffolk,
experimenting with radio waves sent out over
the sea, but by February 1936 they needed
new premises and moved further down the
Suffolk coast to a manor house at Bawdsey
near Felixtowe. Bawdsey Manor House and
its outbuildings, used as a location in the
'Eagle Day' episode, became the birthplace
of Britain's radar air defence system and the
first of the 21 Chain Home Radar Stations.
From these all-important installations, details

ABOVE: *Britain's air-defence radar stations were priority targets for the German bombers when they began their* Aldertag *or 'Eagle Day' offensive in August 1940.*

of the height and speed of approaching enemy aircraft were sent to Fighter Command Headquarters at Bentley Priory in Stanmore, then on to the different Fighter Group HQs and finally to specific fighter airfields. Because it was a non-combatant role and the manpower shortage had led to women being drafted into the RAF as WAAFs, many of the radar operators were female, just as is depicted in 'Eagle Day'. The Germans knew of the existence of radar, the radar stations and masts becoming the first targets on *Aldertag* or 'Eagle Day' on 12 August 1940, when Luftwaffe chief Hermann Göring launched his air offensive against the RAF and began the Battle of Britain. The radar stations were well protected and priority was given to getting them back in operation after an attack. While they were 'down' the Royal Observer Corps, thousands of sky-watchers around the coast, were left to telephone sightings of incoming aircraft to Bentley Priory to try to plug the gaps.

DCS Foyle's murdered man in the bombed building is a scenario also based on real-life incidents such as the one in Kennington Lane, London in July 1942, when workmen demolishing a bombed church discovered a skeleton in the ruins. You could assume that this might not be too unusual in a church, ancient tombs often existing within the walls, but the condition of the body suggested it was more recent. Forensic examination showed that the body was that of a woman who had been strangled, dismembered and buried in lime to accelerate decomposition. Police eventually identified her as Rachel Dobkin and her estranged husband, Harry, was hanged for her murder in January 1943. In another case a witness directed police to a bombed house in Kitchen Street, Liverpool, where they found the body of Gwendoline Sweeney lying in the rubble. Far from having died

in an air raid, she had been strangled and stabbed. Thomas James, who had been seen in her company on the night of her death, was convicted of her murder and hanged in November 1943.

DCS Foyle also has art thefts to contend during the murder investigation in 'Eagle Day'. The idea of removing national treasures to a place of safe storage for the duration of the war is one that was pursued by many institutions, including the National Gallery. Around 3,000 priceless works of art were packed up and sent for storage in a secret underground chamber at the Manod Quarry near Blaenau Ffestiniog in Wales. Art treasures were not the only valuables to be transported for safe keeping, although it would have taken an audacious thief to have tried to steal the gold and securities valued at hundreds of millions (£billions in today's terms) that were sent by warship to the Bank of Canada in Montreal from the Bank of England in July 1940.

Fifty Ships

Set in September 1940, while the Battle of Britain still raged overhead, 'Fifty Ships' sees the boarding house where Sam lived destroyed by a bomb. Her friend dies in the blast and the building is badly damaged. In a sinister turn of events, it transpires that Sam's landlady has lost property looted from the building and the Auxiliary Fire Service volunteers who had attended the blast fall under suspicion. The father of one of the firemen later dies on the beach in an apparent suicide not far from where Foyle is having dinner with an old friend, Arthur Lewes and his wife Elizabeth, with whom Foyle himself was at one time romantically linked. Among the other dinner guests are the Lewes' neighbours Alan and Eve Redmond, as well as Howard Paige, an American industrialist heavily engaged in

ABOVE: *The Spitfire is one of the most famous aircraft ever to have flown. The first RAF Spitfire was delivered to 19 Squadron at Duxford in August 1938 and by the time production ceased, 20,000 of various types had been produced.*

LEFT: *Foyle with Elizabeth, his first love, who complied with her father's wish for her not to marry Foyle, yet subsequently named her second son, Christopher, after him.*

high-level discussions about what would become the Lend-Lease deal that would allow the United States to supply war aid to Britain. This is from where the episode's title, 'Fifty Ships', is derived. The first aid that President Roosevelt's government actually supplied came in the form of 50 outdated destroyers. The scheme was a way for neutral America (prior to the December 1941 Japanese attack on Pearl Harbor) to help the Allied cause in a way that those Americans against any US involvement in the war could not oppose. In return for the 'Fifty Ships' and the subsequent $50 billion of arms, equipment and food that America supplied to the Allies, America was given leases on land throughout the British Empire on which to build military bases. Opinions in America were polarised by the war. The Committee to Defend America by Aiding the Allies (CDAAA) supported intervention, but the America First Committee (AFC), which included a young John F. Kennedy, fellow future President Gerald R. Ford and Charles Lindbergh among its supporters, was for isolationism. In the end, the Japanese resolved the argument for them.

Back on the beach in 'Fifty Ships', the suicide turns into a murder investigation when Foyle is tipped off by the strangest of witnesses – a German spy who has been paddling ashore in a small boat. He is arrested the following morning after arousing suspicion by trying to order beer in a pub first thing in the morning. The spy illuminates the circumstances of the death on the darkened beach but still has to face the gallows, unlike the murderer who slips through Foyle's fingers, thanks to some frustrating high-level political interference.

Sadly, looting was an all-too-common occurrence during the bombings of World War II. The story Sam told in 'Fifty Ships' about a woman trapped unconscious in the wreckage of her home waking up to feel someone trying to wrench her wedding ring off her finger is a true tale from The Blitz. The emergency services were certainly among those involved in looting and ARP personnel were imprisoned for the offence in October 1940. There were almost 400 cases of looting in London during the first two months of The Blitz, with members of the Auxiliary Fire Service (AFS) among the perpetrators, just as portrayed in 'Fifty Ships.' The cases were not, however, all the kind of cynical crimes portrayed in *Foyle's War.* When shops were bombed, goods ended up scattered in the street, lying there for the taking as you walked past. But if stopped by a policeman as you headed home, having picked up a watch, or a pair of shoes, you could easily be arrested for being a looter. Looting became such a problem in the capital that an anti-looting squad of 300 officers was formed to combat the phenomenon.

The penalty for looting was, officially, capital punishment – you could be hanged. In an attempt to discourage looters, notices to this effect were posted on buildings and the sentences imposed by the courts became more and more severe, although they stopped short of hanging. For carrying off two buckets of food from a shattered grocery shop, an Auxiliary Fireman was sentenced to five years' penal servitude in 1940. That

sentence was later revoked on appeal, but it demonstrated how seriously the problem was taken. Several people found themselves in court for looting coal. When St Mark's Church in Holloway was bombed three people were arrested for sifting through the debris to collect lumps of coal. A widow in south London was prosecuted and fined for taking coal from her next-door neighbour's house after it had been destroyed by a bomb.

There were, of course, more deliberate, callous looters. Professional thieves raided the houses of those who had been evacuated not only from the major cities but also from coastal towns like Dover where vans, painted in the liveries of local firms so as not to attract attention, were driven into town empty and driven out again laden with the entire contents of evacuees' homes. In Southend-

ABOVE: *Arthur Lewes (Nicholas Le Provost) was the man Elizabeth eventually did marry, the ambitious young lawyer being seen by her father as far more suitable than Foyle, the lowly son of a policeman.*

ABOVE: *A German spy was Foyle's prize witness in a murder investigation in 'Fifty Ships' but, despite identifying the culprit, Foyle was forced to watch him board a plane and flee to America.*

on-Sea by July 1941 more than two dozen prosecutions were brought against thieves who had stolen from the homes of evacuees.

The police, unfortunately, were not always blameless when it came to looting. One young officer's career ended when he was guarding a site where an aircraft had crashed into a photography shop in Highbury, north London. He pocketed a camera that was lying on the ground. He should, of course, have resisted the temptation, but his crime was nowhere near as shocking as the officers of Folkestone Borough Police who copied the organised gangs and burgled unoccupied houses around the town.

Far less accomplished than the looters who lurked in the darkness were the German

spies infiltrated onto the British mainland. According to MI5, German documents captured after the war was over showed that more than 100 German agents were in Britain, or sent to Britain during the war, and all of them were identified and caught except one. The one who got away only did so by committing suicide before he could be captured. Hans Maier, the would-be spy encountered by Foyle in 'Fifty Ships', is based on Carl Meier, a Dutch subject who landed by dinghy from a fishing boat, along with Jose Waldberg, a German, on 3 September 1940. They came ashore under cover of night at Dungeness in Kent, hid their radio and batteries, and then settled down for a sleep. Early the next morning Waldberg requested that Meier (the best English speaker) should walk into Lydd, where he could buy something to drink and some cigarettes. With no knowledge of English licensing laws, his first port of call was a pub where he asked for some cider. The landlady explained that she couldn't serve him just yet and recommended that he take a look around the town. When he came back it would be time. When he came back, of course, the landlady had summoned help and Meier was taken to Lydd police station. Waldberg was picked up the next day. Two other agents, Kieboom and Pons, who had crossed the channel on the same vessel as Meier and Waldberg, had landed at Romney Marsh near Hythe and were captured by a Private Tollervey of the Somerset Light Infantry within minutes of coming ashore. Waldberg and Meier were hanged on 10 December 1940 and Kieboom followed them to the gallows a week later. Pons was, like Kieboom and Meier, Dutch and was found not guilty of spying as the jury accepted that he had been forced by the Germans to undertake the mission.

A more traditional spy was Josef Jakobs, a German soldier who was parachuted into England in 1941 along with his radio, a wad of cash, some brandy and a German sausage. He was arrested by the Home Guard before he had been on British soil for more than 12 hours. Sentenced to death at his trial, he had the honour of being the only spy to be executed by firing squad at the Tower of London during World War II.

Lord Jowitt, as Solicitor-General from June 1940 until March 1942, had the task of prosecuting spies brought to court. He regarded the German efforts at espionage as astoundingly amateurish and wrote in his 1954 book, *Some Were Spies*:

The cases of which I had experience bore all the marks of hasty and very imperfect improvisation, and it seems surprising if, indeed the Germans had any better organisation – that they should have resorted to such crude methods.

LEFT: *Howard Paige (Henry Goodman) was the wealthy American industrialist who committed murder yet slipped through Foyle's fingers due to political interference.*

Among The Few

Foyle and Sam almost come to grief in 'Among The Few' when they are fired upon by a thug in a speeding truck. The truck has broken through a Home Guard roadblock checkpoint where Foyle has stopped to show his identification. Unfortunately for the gunman, when Sam and Foyle give chase he loses control of the truck and crashes, burning alive when his cargo of stolen fuel catches light.

When Foyle decides to look into the circumstances surrounding the fuel theft, he reluctantly agrees to let Sam go to work undercover as a tanker driver at a fuel depot. Sam befriends one of the other women drivers, Connie, and escorts her to the Flamingo Club, where Connie seems on very good terms with Frank Gannon, the owner. They also encounter Andrew Foyle, now on active service with a fighter squadron, and a group of his RAF pilot friends. Sam is on the verge of discovering the source of the fuel thefts when the investigation takes a sinister turn: Connie is murdered. The investigation becomes a delicate one for Foyle when it transpires that Connie was romantically involved with Andrew's closest friend – and perhaps even Andrew himself. The villainous Frank Gannon becomes part of Foyle's investigation, as does Sean O'Halloran, who attempts to destroy evidence of the fuel thefts by planting a bomb at the fuel depot intended to look like an IRA attack. Luckily for Sam who is trapped inside the building, the bomb is disarmed before it detonates.

Given that most ordinary people had little use for petrol during the war, with only 'essential users' given a petrol ration, you

ABOVE: *Sam returned to more regular MTC duties when she went undercover to investigate a petrol scam in 'Among The Few'.*

LEFT: *Foyle's investigation into the petrol racket ultimately involved not only Sam but also his son when it transpired that one of Andrew's RAF chums was romantically involved with Connie, a tanker driver.*

might think that petrol theft as portrayed in 'Among The Few' would be fairly limited. For the villains, after all, it was not like stealing razor blades, cigarettes or clothing coupons, which could be sold on in nightclubs or street markets. Petrol is awkward, smelly stuff that can't easily be passed under the counter. So why would anyone choose to try to steal it?

The answer is to think big. The essential users generally needed as much petrol as they could get. Sam would have needed to keep the petrol tank of Foyle's Wolesley topped up, but the car would not have used a huge amount of fuel. The real consumers were those who ran commercial vehicles, or fleets of trucks, and one of the biggest petrol scandals of the war involved two major construction firms, Sir Alexander Gibbs & Co and Sir Lindsay Parkinson and Co. An investigation into their activities in Lancashire was conducted by the Petroleum Board's Chief Petroleum Inspector for the north-west, Arthur Fox. Mr Fox discovered that the two companies had been acquiring black market petrol for themselves and their subcontractors, and even selling the fuel on to other companies, all vastly in excess of the amounts to which they were entitled.

Arthur Fox's efforts saw the firms being brought to court in 1941, facing prosecutions for buying and handling petrol in contravention of the Motor Fuel Rationing Order to the tune of 145,000 gallons. Clever defence lawyers tried to argue that, because the companies were officially contracted to the Ministry of Supply, they should not be prosecuted as they were, technically, on government business and were 'agents of the Crown'. As such they should be immune from

ABOVE: *Sam was close to uncovering the petrol scam when the case turned into a murder investigation with tanker driver Connie Dewar (Lisa Kay) the victim.*

ABOVE: *Sean O'Halloran (Damian O'Hare) was an Irish engineer with links to the IRA who had designs on Connie and planted a bomb that almost killed Sam.*

prosecution. When this defence was thrown out, attention began to focus on Arthur Fox.

It transpired that Mr Fox was not the form-filling, paperclip-counting, lifelong civil servant he may first have appeared. He was one of the 'new boys' taken on as an administrator when the minefield of rationing legislation was introduced. He had come, as had so many others, clutching appropriate references straight from the Labour Exchange. And, as happened from time to time, Mr Fox's background was not assiduously researched, although once it became known, no one could maintain that it was in any way contiguous with the position of trust and integrity to which he had been appointed. Prior to working for the Petroleum Board, Mr Fox had run a theatrical agency with his wife. Neither was this his first visit to a court of law. He had been prosecuted only a couple of years

before for running his theatrical agency without the appropriate license. On that occasion, witnesses testified Mr Fox had tried to persuade some of his female clients to take work in Brazil. This was a practice that had become a scandal in itself in the late thirties when stories of a 'white slave trade' emerged, with girls shipped to South America for immoral purposes.

Mr Fox could not deny these allegations. Neither could he deny that, far from having led the life one might expect of a responsible public servant, he had run up bad gambling debts, been managing director of company that had gone bankrupt and opened bank accounts using a number of false names. Even before his dubious past was revealed, there were questions being asked about his conduct at the Petroleum Board. Documents pertaining to other investigations he was handling had vanished under mysterious circumstances. The press had a field day reporting on the 'white slave trader' working for a government department.

The case against the construction firms still went ahead but with the main prosecution witness having proved to be so unreliable, the fines they received were not as punitive as they might have been. Questions were asked in the House of Commons about the curious Mr Fox who was sacked from the Petroleum Board as soon as the court case ended.

Big business, then, could be into big petrol scams during the period of rationing, justifying the petrol theft storyline in 'Among The Few,' but what about the IRA bomb that almost brought a premature end to Sam's sleuthing career? How active was the IRA during World War II?

The IRA had declared war on Britain long before Britain declared war on Germany. As the prospect of war with Germany loomed ever closer, the IRA issued a proclamation purporting to come from the Irish Government. The statement came on 12 January 1939 and warned that, unless British troops were removed from Northern Ireland (the south having been independent of Great Britain since 1922) within four

days and the British Government relinquish all claims on the territory, war would be declared. On 16 January, their ultimatum having been ignored, the IRA launched their campaign on mainland Britain by attempting to disrupt electricity supplies, blowing up pylons and sub-stations. One man was killed in Manchester during these attacks but within two days police had rounded up the eight-man IRA active service unit in charge of the Manchester arms cache and within two weeks Special Branch were in possession of the republicans' 'S-Plan', the blueprint for their British atrocities.

Yet still the attacks came. Victoria and King's Cross stations in London were targeted, as was Hammersmith Bridge. Two men were later given penal servitude sentences of 10 and 20 years for trying to blow up the Bridge. Despite claims that they had been trained by a German sabotage expert, they failed to destroy it, lacking the technical knowledge about how best to place their charges to weaken the structure. Many of the other IRA bombs failed to detonate because they were poorly made, their alarm-clock timers simply failing to go off.

RIGHT: *The Flamingo Club was the place where Andrew Foyle's RAF crowd liked to let their hair down but was also the centre of operations for the villainous Frank Gannon (Justin Salinger).*

The worst of the bombings happened on 25 August 1939 at Broadgate in Coventry, where there would later be so much devastation as a result of German air raids. The Broadgate bomb was not the first IRA device to go off in the city, but it was the most vicious. It was placed in a bicycle shopping basket and the bicycle left on the pavement in the busy shopping area. It went off at 2.30 pm, killing council worker Gwilym Rowland, 80-year-old James Clay, office worker Rex Gentle, 15-year-old shop assistant John Corbett and 21-year-old bride-to-be Elsie Ansell, and injuring 50 passers-by. Several arrests were made within 24 hours and two men were ultimately found guilty of the bombing. Peter Barnes and James Richards were hanged on 7 February 1940, Barnes justifying the bombing in court as being part of the struggle for Irish freedom and ending his address with 'God Bless Ireland.'

The last of this wave of bombings came in March 1940, the IRA having by then run out of funds despite raids on Post Offices and Banks in Dublin, stealing from the people for whom they claimed to be fighting. They were also weakened by the fact that many known IRA members being interned in Ulster. IRA leader Sean Russell had travelled to America to try to find support and finance for their 'war' in September 1939 but was expelled by the US Government. He then travelled to Germany, hoping to forge links there but, although the Germans undoubtedly appreciated the nuisance value of the IRA as a thorn in the side of the British, they tended to regard the republicans at that time as an amateurish 'army'. Unfortunately for Russell he fell ill while being shipped to Ireland on a U-boat, after attending meetings in Berlin, and died. He was afforded the respect of a military burial at sea, his body wrapped in a German flag.

ABOVE: *Not the work of the Luftwaffe, but of an IRA active service unit that detonated a bomb in a busy area of Coventry at the end of August 1939, less than two weeks before Britain declared war on Germany.*

War Games

A death in London when a young woman falls from a tall building, the headquarters of a multinational conglomerate, is not something to trouble DCS Foyle down in Hastings, even if the woman's death may have been murder. Foyle is occupied in investigating a burglary at the country home of wealthy industrialist Sir Reginald Walker, although he is suspicious that the ransacked house may have played host to something more sinister than a mere break-in. His attention is drawn elsewhere, however, when he is called upon to act as a referee in a major series of Home Guard manoeuvres, but he quickly reverts to his role as a detective when a member of the Home Guard is killed. Was this a tragic accident or might there have been a motive behind the killing of the part-time soldier? Looking into the man's death draws Foyle into a tangled web of intrigue involving high finance and a corporation that saw no need to curtail its foreign operations and international deals simply because it meant having to deal with the Nazis.

Such was the spread in the 1930s of what might nowadays be termed 'globalisation' that major industrial organisations all over Europe and in America were linked, if not in the actual physical production of goods, then certainly through investment banks and other financial institutions. Prescott Bush, grandfather of President George W Bush, was investigated for 'trading with the enemy' during World War II. A number of businesses and financial organisations with which he was involved continued their association with their German partners not only after Britain went to war in 1939, but also after America entered the war at the end of 1941.

Large American multinational manufacturers such as General Motors or IBM had facilities in Europe that continued to operate after the countries in which they

ABOVE: *Foyle chats with his German-born friend Stephen Beck (Alan Howard), a naturalised Briton and lawyer involved with the intelligence services.*

were based were taken over by the Nazis. Accusations have been levelled against IBM that it continued to trade with the Germans via its Swiss office well into the war. The punch-card data systems made by IBM were used by the Germans to organise the hugely complicated rail networks throughout Europe but it has been alleged that the systems were also used to maintain records for the Nazi persecution of the Jews. It is, perhaps, difficult to imagine why an organisation like IBM should shoulder the blame for its machines being used by the Germans any more than the Ford Motor Company could be blamed for allowing vehicles from its European plants to be built for the Nazis.

In the case of Ford's involvement, however, there is another factor to take into account when considering their trade links with the Nazis. The founder of the corporation, Henry Ford, was an influential force in the America First movement, determined to keep America out of the war in Europe. He also held strong anti-Semitic views, which he expressed through a newspaper he owned in Detroit and in a

ABOVE: *Foyle and Milner leave the country home of business magnate Sir Reginald Baker, where Foyle suspects that a simple burglary may not have been as simple as it seems.*

LEFT: *Stephen Beck with the mysterious Hilda Pierce (Ellie Haddington). They clearly shared an intriguing past and had their own ideas about how to help the war effort.*

pamphlet he published in the 1920s entitled 'The International Jew'. Hitler was a great admirer of Henry Ford, who is said to have made large donations to the Nazi party during its rise to power, and on Ford's 75th birthday in July 1938 he was awarded the Grand Cross of the Supreme Order of the German Eagle. This was the highest honour that could be awarded to any non-German citizen and Ford was the first ever American on whom it was bestowed.

The Ford plant in Cologne, today the company's largest facility in Europe, made vehicles for the German military during the war, as did their plant in France. Ford's headquarters in Dearborn remained in contact with their European operations long after the war began and even after America became involved. The company was in no way responsible, of course, for the slave labour that was used in the Cologne works, some of the forced labour even coming from Buchenwald concentration camp. Naturally, no company could be expected simply to shut down its foreign operations when war threatened. The situation for most was very quickly beyond their control and Ford was no more able

to cease production at Cologne than the Allies were to bomb the factory out of existence. But there was still a fine line to be walked between satisfying shareholders' interests and the treasonous act of trading with the enemy.

The Home Guard operations in the 'War Games' episode look strangely professional to anyone brought up with the slapstick comedy of the TV series *Dad's Army*, but the real Dad's Army was no joke. The volunteers, some of whom worked in reserved occupations all day and then turned out four nights a week with their platoon to patrol their local area or man roadblocks, were well aware of the seriousness of the task they faced if an invasion should come. Although there were few weapons with which to supply the Home Guard when they were first established in May 1940, 500,000 rifles, 190 million rounds of ammunition and 80,000 machine guns were soon on their way from America under the Lend-Lease agreement. The Home Guard were expected not only to guard installations, keep watch for enemy parachutists, downed fliers and spies, but also tackle the spearhead units of an advancing German army, should it come. Pitting part-time soldiers, old men and boys against battle-hardened German shock troops might seem like madness, but their jobs at crossroads machine-gun nests, pillboxes by bridges or roadside ambush points was to harass the enemy, delaying their advance. This was to allow the regular army time to mount a more effective defence at one of their prepared 'stop-lines'.

One Home Guard corporal on the Isle of Wight, John Graham, fully realised that he and his friends stood no chance against the Germans. He expected that they would 'put up a good show for about half a day. And then that would be the end of us.'[2] The British high command thought the same: the Home Guard were expendable. Perhaps as a propaganda exercise to shake their morale, Hitler also expressed an opinion. He viewed the Home Guard as armed civilian guerillas and as such they would be shot if captured when his army invaded England. That, of course, only strengthened the resolve of the Dad's Army.

BELOW: *By the time of the 'War Games' investigation, Sam had gone up in Foyle's estimation to become a valued member of his team.*

[2] *WWII: The People's Story*, Michael O'Mara Books for Reader's Digest 2003

The Funk Hole

As the night bombing Blitz on London intensifies during October 1940, Foyle becomes involved in investigations into the theft of food from a ministry depot in Hastings, during which the Home Guard soldiers on guard at the depot open fire on the thieves. The disappearance of a young man, Matthew Farley, becomes a major concern when it appears he might have been one of the thieves shot by the guards.

Foyle's attempts to locate him lead to a hotel called Brookfield Court, where Farley worked on a casual basis. At Brookfield there is a strange assortment of guests in residence, playing tennis and relaxing in comfort, seemingly oblivious to the war that embroils the rest of the country. Milner describes the place as a 'Funk Hole,' where people who can afford to pay for such comforts shelter from the inconveniences of the war. Farley's body is discovered in the woods close to Brookfield and Foyle's interest in the place intensifies just as he is taken off the case, suspended while under investigation for allegedly spreading dissent on a recent trip to London. The accusation is that he has been heard in an air-raid shelter, telling anyone who will listen that he is with the police, and that 'The Jerries have won and we might as well pack up!' One of the residents at Brookfield subsequently dies under suspicious circumstances and the bombing of a London school that is being used as a shelter for families who had lost their homes ultimately provides Foyle with the solution to the Brookfield murder and his own salvation.

The term 'funk hole' dates back to World War I when it was a phrase used to describe a safe bunker in the trenches where a man could hide if he was 'in a funk' or afraid. During World War II it was used as a derogatory term for the kind of hotel or guest house deep in the safety of the countryside that offered wealthy people a chance to escape from the war-torn cities. Although at the outbreak of the war the government had actually encouraged people who were able to leave the cities to find somewhere safe to stay, it wasn't long before the rich refugees had to endure a barrage of criticism. *The Times* found itself in the peculiar position of both aiding the flight of the rich and condemning them for doing so. Advertisements placed in the newspaper's classified section offered a farmhouse in Suffolk or a furnished cottage in the Chilterns under the heading ARP (Air Raid Precautions). In September 1940,

ABOVE: *Frank Vaudrey (Richard Hope) had fled from London to live in the safety of the Brookfield Court 'funk hole' – but harboured a dark secret.*

ABOVE: *Colin Fowler (Richard McCabe) spread doom and gloom in a London air raid shelter, causing no end of problems for Foyle in Hastings.*

a year after the war began and with British cities facing nightly visits by the Luftwaffe, an advertisement in *The Times* tempted those who could afford it with the thought of a peaceful night's sleep in Torquay: 'You can sleep at the Grand Hotel for the drone of an aero engine is rare and sirens even more infrequent'. There was also the comfort of the Queen's Hotel in Penzance where 'a sense of security cannot be beaten'.

In contrast to its classified ads, by January 1941 *The Times'* editorial comments were pitched against the funk holes and those who inhabited them. At a time when conscription was being extended, rationing was biting hard and people in the cities were suffering real privation, *The Times* snarled that 'the hotels are filled with well-to-do refugees, who too often have fled from nothing. They sit and read, and knit and eat and drink, and get no nearer the war than the news they read in the papers.'

Of course, the aristocracy, who owned country estates, always had the option of fleeing from war-torn London (providing their houses had not been requisitioned by the military), but the finest example was set by the King and Queen. They remained in London even when the government urged that the Queen and the royal princesses should move out to the country, to Scotland or even to Canada. 'The princesses cannot go without me,' the Queen famously stated, 'I cannot go without the King and the King will never leave.' They remained in London throughout The Blitz, doing their best to boost the morale of Londoners and the nation. Perhaps their images in the newspapers made those funk hole beds seem a little less comfortable to those who had fled.

One of the characters in 'The Funk Hole' episode is hiding out at the hotel, evading conscription. Laying low like that was really the last option for those who wanted to try to avoid military service. It was

a theme introduced in the very first episode of *Foyle's War* when DCS Foyle goes out on his first case with Sam as his driver. Foyle has arranged to meet a man by the tall huts on the shingle beach at Hastings and during their conversation it becomes clear that the man (who identifies himself as Keegan, a civil servant in Brighton) can make call-up papers disappear. When Foyle explains he is trying to make sure his son doesn't have to go to war, the man assures him a charge of £150 is all that it takes. Foyle then identifies himself as a police officer and arrests Keegan but he makes a run for it, only to be laid out when Sam smacks him in the face with a dustbin lid.

There were, of course, real officials during the war who were willing to offer the kind of service for which the fictional Keegan is arrested. One official from the Ministry of Labour in south London, Wilfred Bailey, accepted £200 from one man for making sure his conscription documents never saw the light of day. He received a six-month prison sentence in December 1942.

The resident murdered at Brookfield Court turns out to be a local councillor from London, who has been one of those responsible for evacuating a group of people left homeless by The Blitz. Foyle mentions early on in the episode that the civil administration in London is on the verge of collapse and many local councils perfectly competent during peacetime were struggling to cope during the destruction of the air raids. The fictional councillor at Brookfield was part of an administration that had packed homeless people into a local school to await evacuation only for the school to be destroyed by a bomb. This is based on the story of South Hallsville School in Canning Town, London. In 1940 the school was being used as a reception and transit centre with hundreds of people, mainly women and children, crowded inside. They were provided

ABOVE: *When Foyle was suspended from duty, John Collier (Nicholas Farrell) was the officer sent to replace him, although he had his own motives for doing so.*

with blankets but very little food was given to them as they waited for buses to take them out of the city. The buses promised by the council never came, and on 10 September, as the people settled in for another miserable night in the school, the building was destroyed by a bomb. The official death toll was 73, but locals believe it may have been as high as 450. Next day the buses arrived.

The French Drop

At the beginning of 'The French Drop' Foyle is hopeful of being able to leave the police force and find a position where he can satisfy his desire to make a more direct commitment to the war effort. He is tired of arresting shopkeepers for overcharging or dealing in black market goods, and asks his brother-in-law at the Admiralty if he can pull some strings to try to get him drafted into naval intelligence. That, however, is before Foyle begins investigating the bizarre death of a young man apparently blown up with a hand grenade. A watch found on the body is traced to William Messenger, the son of Sir Giles Messenger, a major player in MI6. Sir Giles' son, it transpires, has joined what Sir Giles views as a rival new covert organisation, SOE. Foyle's investigation into the death of William Messenger takes him to an SOE training camp where he unravels a long, intricately-woven curtain of deception that conceals not a murder but yet another deception, a smokescreen created to cover up professional incompetence. Foyle proves there has been no murder but in doing so he incurs the wrath of Sir Giles, which compromises his own efforts to join the intelligence community.

ABOVE: *Ever hopeful of finding a role in which he could better contribute to the war effort, Foyle enlisted the help of his brother-in-law, Commander Howard (Rupert Frazer), to try to secure a position in Naval Intelligence.*

ABOVE: *Sir Giles Messenger (Ronald Pickup), a senior officer with MI6, was deeply suspicious of the other intelligence organisations and took an instant dislike to Foyle.*

The professional jealousy and personal rivalry of those involved in the spy game in 'The French Drop' may make it seem as though those involved were making the fighting of the war a lot more difficult and complicated than it needed to be, but in reality there was little love lost between the different agencies as they competed for resources, each one anxious to protect its own operatives and networks, to maintain its own regime. There is often some confusion over what the different branches of Britain's intelligence service are called, and the agencies have changed their names several times since they were first created.

A review of Britain's counter-espionage capabilities was conducted in 1909 at a time when Britain and Germany were involved in an arms race, creating huge naval fleets to compete for dominance on the high seas. The British authorities were concerned about the vulnerability of Britain's ports to German spies. Spy fever was sweeping the country, with reports of sightings of suspected spies appearing in the popular press and rewards offered by the media for information about German secret agents. In conjunction with the War Office, the Admiralty decided to set up a Secret Service Bureau to handle the gathering of intelligence. The task of organising the new department was given to Captain Kell of the South Staffordshire Regiment, and the Royal Navy's Captain Cumming. The two men were also asked to find out anything they could about the new ships being built for the German navy. Kell and Cumming opted for a division of labour, with Kell handling counter-espionage on the home front and Cumming taking on the task of intelligence gathering abroad.

Kell's Home Section of the Secret Service Bureau became part of the War Office's

LEFT: *Sir Giles and Lady Messenger (Angela Thorne) lost their son when he was killed during an SOE mission that went disastrously wrong.*

Directorate of Military Operations section 5 and was given the name MO5(g). This became MI5 (Military Intelligence section 5) during World War I. It was later renamed the Defence Security Service and, in 1931, the Security Service, which is the name it still uses today. Cumming's part of the organisation also went through several name changes including MI1(c), Special Intelligence Service and, from the 1920s onwards, the Secret Intelligence Service (SIS), the title it still uses. During World War II, however, the title MI6 was often used, especially during joint operations with MI5, even though MI5 no longer used that term.

It was into this world of evolving organisations and structures that the SOE was born in July 1940. With the Allied armies having been defeated on mainland Europe, Churchill wanted to find as many ways as possible to carry the war to the enemy rather than fighting it on our own doorstep. Hugh Dalton, the Minister for Economic Warfare,

suggested setting up a new organisation to help local groups within German-occupied territories commit acts of sabotage and espionage. Churchill gave the go-ahead for the formation of the SOE with the now-famous phrase, 'And now set Europe ablaze!'

The established intelligence services were wholly unsure about the creation of this new outfit and the regular forces even less enthusiastic. One senior Air Force officer expressed his distaste at having to deliver men by parachute into enemy territory, who were not dressed in uniform and ready to fight, but were sneaking in as assassins. Nevertheless, the selection and training of agents forged ahead. SOE staff originally operated from an office in Baker Street in London, from where their nickname, the 'Baker Street Irregulars' comes. But training camps were established at Wanborough Manor near Guildford in Surrey as well as Beaulieu Manor in the New Forest and a number of locations in the wilds of Scotland.

Recruits were taught unarmed combat, radio skills, sabotage techniques and, of course, how to use all manner of guns and explosive devices. The SOE even developed its own special 'toys' such as exploding rats or camel dung, shoes that left false footprints, submersible canoes or shaving cream tubes with hidden compartments. During the war 470 agents were sent into France where they faced the constant danger of being discovered, betrayed or captured. Once in the hands of the Gestapo they faced gruesome torture but were trained to hold out for two days, during which time everyone else in their local network could make good their escape.

But it was not only men who were selected as SOE agents. In 1940 Yvonne Cormeau's husband was killed in an air raid. She joined the WAAF but, having been born in China and educated in Brussels and Edinburgh, she spoke fluent French as well as Spanish and German. Once her psychological suitability had been assessed, she was snapped up for SOE training. In 1943 she was dropped into occupied France. Below her jumpsuit she wore a black coat and skirt along with a white blouse. He ankles were bandaged as she wore shoes, not jump boots. For many months Yvonne's specialist skill as a radio operator was put to good use. She lived among people who hated the Germans, but whose personal or family vendettas could often lead to betrayal. Yvonne worked with a local network in the Gironde and, despite one underhand attempt to identify her to the Gestapo and several close shaves as the Germans desperately tried to trace her radio, she was never captured.

BELOW: *Both the SOE and MI6 had agents in the field throughout Europe, keeping track of some of them using operational charts like this one, pieced together from smaller, detailed maps of each area.*

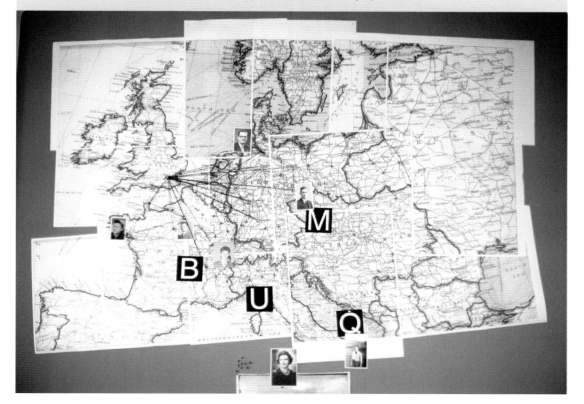

Enemy Fire

World War I veteran Sir Michael Waterford and his housekeeper, Mrs Roecastle, are not best pleased when Sir Michael's home, Digby Manor House, is taken over by the military and earmarked to house a special hospital unit for wounded airmen. When the unit eventually moves in, it turns out to be not a rest and recuperation centre but a surgical facility run by the brilliant, but unorthodox surgeon Patrick Jamieson. His methods are as advanced as his attitude unconventional. Jamieson eschews military discipline and uniforms, and runs the hospital more like a club. Foyle is called upon to investigate when it becomes apparent that someone is attempting to sabotage their work and force the closure of the unit. Andrew Foyle becomes part of the equation when a flight mechanic, Drake, with whom he had a heated argument over the maintenance of his Spitfire is found murdered. The mechanic, it transpires, is quite familiar with Digby Manor prior to the arrival of Jamieson's medical unit, and has also been having an affair with the wife of a doctor on Jamieson's staff. Foyle has no shortage of suspects, especially since a young pilot sent on a mission in Andrew's plane crashes and is badly burned, becoming one of Jamieson's patients due to Drake's negligence. When Andrew Foyle disappears, it seems he might have to be added to the list of suspects, too.

The story of the burns unit set up by Patrick Jamieson in 'Enemy Fire' takes its inspiration from the work of groundbreaking surgeon Archibald McIndoe. Born in New Zealand in 1900, McIndoe studied medicine at Otago University before working as a surgeon at Waihato Hospital. He then spent some time conducting research and working in America before heading for London in 1930. McIndoe worked in the plastic surgery department at St Bartholomew' Hospital, and lectured at the Hospital for Tropical Diseases until he obtained a Fellowship of the American College of Surgeons in 1934. Four years later he was appointed the RAF's consultant in plastic surgery. On 4 September 1939, McIndoe arrived at the Queen Victoria Hospital in East Grinstead, West Sussex, with instructions to establish

LEFT: *The work of the RAF ground crews was essential to getting fighter aircraft back in the air as quickly as possible and sub-standard repairs like those discovered by Andrew Foyle were not tolerated.*

ABOVE: *The faulty cockpit canopy on Andrew's Spitfire failed to open when his friend crash-landed in the aircraft, trapping him in the burning wreckage.*

a specialist treatment centre for casualties suffering from facial injuries and burns.

In order to give them the best possible range and endurance, combat aircraft carried as much fuel as possible. Both of the RAF's most modern fighter planes, the Spitfire and the Hurricane, had fuel tanks situated directly in front of the pilot's cockpit. If the tanks were ruptured in action, the pilot could easily be sprayed with flaming aviation fuel. The horrific burns suffered by some of the pilots were treated at East Grinstead with pioneering techniques developed by McIndoe almost on a case-by-case basis. In the full knowledge that they were undergoing experimental procedures, the pilots came to refer to themselves as McIndoe's 'guinea pigs' and formed an association called The Guinea Pig Club. McIndoe himself was not afforded such a disrespectful nickname among his patients. Instead they referred to him as 'Boss' or 'Maestro'.

McIndoe fought the physical aspects of his patients' wounds, battling infection and the rejection of skin grafts, and putting some of his patients through over 30 operations during their stay at East Grinstead. But he also recognised that they had psychological problems to face in coming to terms with their disfigurement. He built them new lips and gave them new eyelids or skin grafts that would allow them to use their hands again, but he could not make them look exactly like the dashing young pilots they once were. Working with his good friends Neville and Elaine Blond, McIndoe began to persuade local people to accept patients into their homes. In this way he could help the airmen adjust to the outside world. They were not often seen by members of the public, but being out in the real world helped them to stop feeling so isolated. McIndoe did not want the airmen to feel they were being kept away from the very people they had fought to protect. Getting the guinea pigs back into circulation, even in a small way, also helped them to come to terms with the way people reacted to their injuries. Inside the specialist unit he deliberately kept the atmosphere as relaxed as possible. The facility came under the authority of the RAF, but McIndoe never wore a uniform and did not expect his patients to do so either. He wanted them to feel like people, rather than prisoners.

As the war progressed, McIndoe had more patients from bomber crews than he did from fighter squadrons, with 80 per cent of his guinea pigs in the last year of the war having sustained their injuries on bomber operations. By the end of the war there were 649 members of The Guinea Pig Club. They organised a reunion each year in East Grinstead, some continuing to return for treatment, and continued to do so even after McIndoe died in 1960. Although there are fewer members each year, the club is still in existence today.

ABOVE: *Tom Jackson (Joe Armstrong) was involved in a web of intrigue centred around his father's farm.*

They Fought In The Fields

A German aircraft crashes in the countryside near Hastings. Foyle and Milner, along with the Home Guard members guarding the site, view the wreckage. The body of one German is found nearby, his parachute having failed to open, and there is one dead airman still in the wreckage. Two more are reported to have landed by parachute, leaving Foyle perplexed when told the aircraft is usually manned by a crew of three. Furthermore, it seems the two missing airmen returned to the wreckage of the plane after getting clear. When they are captured, they are handed over to Major Cornwall, as is yet another flier, later found with his parachute caught in a tree. Foyle would have preferred to interview this particular airman in detail as his pistol is missing and a local farmer has been found shot dead.

The dead man was murdered sitting in an armchair in his own farmhouse, the crime having been made to look like suicide. The airman's empty holster means that there is a firearm missing somewhere in the area. The German's Luger pistol eventually turns up at

BELOW: *Barbara Hicks's (Stella Gonet) job in the Land Army was to travel the countryside selecting trees that would be suitable for use as telegraph poles.*

the farm where Sam has been sent to work with some Land Army girls in the hope of picking up information. An intrigue involving illicit love affairs, black market meat and a sinister assassin is soon uncovered.

The girls of the Land Army whom Sam joins for some back-breaking farm work in 'They Fought In The Fields' are doing a job that 90,000 women between the ages of 18 and 40 undertook during the war. Their work in helping to feed the nation was vital, yet those employed in the farming industry were the poorest paid of all industrial workers. The women could expect to earn less than £2 a week, when some women working in factories might make more than three times that amount. They were given less time off than factory workers or service personnel and, even though they were working outdoors in all weathers, they were at the bottom of the list for protective clothing and uniforms. One 18-year-old Land Army girl, Vera Holdstock, found her posting to a farm in Kent 'most exciting', not because of the work but because she could watch the dogfights of the Battle of Britain raging overhead. 'We had a first-class view,' she recalls. 'We used to stand open-mouthed and watch it all.'[3]

The conditions endured by the Land Army volunteers were tempered in many cases by the fact that food was more plentiful

ABOVE: *Romance blossomed for Land Army girl Joan (Jenny Platt) and Hugh Jackson's son Tom, although Hugh (Nigel Terry) was also enjoying a secret affair.*

[3] *WWII: The People's Story*, Michael O'Mara Books for Reader's Digest 2003

in the countryside, so they tended not to go hungry trying to eke out the meagre rations of those trapped in the cities. Perhaps some of them were encouraged to go into agriculture by tales from their mothers or grandmothers, who had fought in the same fields with the Land Army in World War I.

The German specialist from the crashed aircraft in 'They Fought In The Fields' could have been operating a number of different radio direction finding systems developed by the Germans. One was called *Knickebein*, meaning 'crooked leg' and relied on two powerful radio transmitters, one in Germany near the border with Denmark, and one further south near the French border. These transmitters sent out distinct signals and a German bomber could fly into one of the beams and then follow it until it was over England, where the second beam intercepted the first. The crossover point of the two beams was calculated to be over the target, so once the bomber picked up the second signal, the crew knew where to drop their load. Discovered by the British, the system was thwarted by sending out false second signals that caused the bombers to offload miles away from their intended targets.

A more sophisticated system that operated on the same principle, *X-Gerät*, was later developed and used to great effect in bombing raids on Coventry and Birmingham. The only way the British managed to work out how to block *X-Gerät* was when a Heinkel bomber equipped with the system crashed near the English coast and the secret receivers were recovered. It is a fallacy for anyone to think that the Germans knew nothing of the top-secret radar early warning systems that were used to such great effect by the RAF in the Battle of Britain. For years they had been working on their own radar devices for early warning and the targeting of guns prior to the beginning of World War II.

War Of Nerves

A quiet night out in the pub turns out to be a real trial for Sam when a soldier from the bomb disposal unit starts waving a gun around and she bravely steps forward to persuade him to put it down. Foyle, meanwhile, is ordered to keep an eye on a communist agitator, Raymond Carter, who is visiting the town along with his fiancée, painter Lucinda Sheridan. This comes at a time when Foyle and Milner are deep into an investigation into an organised crime gang supplying building materials and equipment to the black market. Milner is even working undercover as a builder, running a business from a fake yard set up by the police. He is offered petrol and other supplies by a man named Ian Kimble, but is shot in the arm when he tries to arrest the man. Kimble works at a local shipyard and when Foyle visits the yard he is suspicious of owners Mark and Peter Talbot, although they appear to co-operate and give him Kimble's home address. This turns out to be non-existent. Kimble is also fictitious, a criminal operating under an assumed name to steal from the shipyard. The yard is then hit during an air raid and an unexploded bomb found on the premises. Jack Archer, his superior Captain Hammond and the third member of their team, Earnest Jones, arrive to defuse the bomb but discover a fortune in cash hidden by the bomb's resting-place and help themselves. It all results in Jones's murder as the men who hid the money torture him to try to make him reveal its location. Foyle's investigation of the murder uncovers a huge fraud at the shipyard as well as the real reason why he is instructed to investigate the communist Raymond Carter.

The kind of fraud perpetrated by the shipyard owners in 'War of Nerves' – claiming wages from the government for 400 workers when their yard actually employed less than half that amount – seems like a far-fetched scenario, but it is based on a scam devised at the Liverpool offices of F. H. Porter Ltd. Following a highly complex investigation a group of conspirators, including a Liverpool City councillor and a naval officer from the Ministry of War Transport, as well as directors and staff of F. H. Porter, was found to have diverted materials intended for the repair of ships to other commercial construction purposes. They were also supplying petrol for private use. But the profits to be made from skimming off petrol and stores were as nothing compared to the money accumulated by charging the Admiralty for wages for 2,000 employees engaged in building ships

for the Royal Navy when really they paid only 800 workers. Around £5,000 was being embezzled in this way every week. Frederick Porter, head of F. H. Porter, ultimately had so much cash tucked away in safety deposit boxes in so many different banks that by the time the case came to court police estimated they had probably only recovered about two-thirds of the money stolen by Mr Porter. This was around £308,000, equivalent to over £12 million today. Frederick Porter was no longer around to help them find the rest, having shot himself on 30 January 1940. The others involved in the operation received sentences ranging from nine months to nine years.

ABOVE: *Milner searches for clues in the bomb-damaged shipyard.*

LEFT: *Ernest Jones (Fergus O'Donnell), Captain Hammond (Dugald Bruce-Lockhart) and Jack Archer (Samuel Oatley) were the bomb disposal crew who found more than just an unexploded device in a local shipyard.*

The Communist figurehead in 'War Of Nerves' whom Foyle is encouraged to keep tabs on – Raymond Carter – is mentioned as one of the leaders of The People's Convention. This was an alliance of left-wing organisations led by the Communist Party demanding a People's Peace and a People's Government. The Communists were against the war with Germany despite the fact that they were also against Fascism. Around half of the 1,500 volunteers of the British Battalion of the International Brigade, who fought the Fascists in Spain during that country's civil war, had been Communists. More than a third were killed. They saw the British Government as being almost as right-wing as the Nazis and, through their strong connections in the trades unions, agitated for workers in industry to strike. Even though strikes had been made illegal in 1940, there were thousands of stoppages in all sectors of industry throughout the war. The majority of these were over pay and conditions rather than being politically motivated. The People's

Convention held its first national conference in London on 12 January 1941 with 2,234 delegates present, who claimed to represent over a million workers. This was, without doubt, a political force to be reckoned with but their stance on the war changed when Germany turned on the Soviet Union in June 1941 and Stalin asked the western powers for military aid. The Communists then began to push for the Allies to attack the Germans from the west in mainland Europe to help their Russian comrades, the People's Peace, then somewhat forgotten.

The work of the Royal Engineers' bomb disposal teams during World War II was incredibly dangerous. With little formal training, the bomb disposal experts learned their craft on the job and, if they were lucky, they were able to learn from others' mistakes. Mistakes, of course, were not something that you lived to regret. The notion of forming bomb disposal units came out of the Spanish Civil War in the later 1930s. This was the first time cities had been bombed from the air in a concerted campaign, and dealing with bombs that failed to detonate became a major problem. British teams, usually consisting of a three-man squad led by an NCO, were hastily put together in 1939. The officer in charge of the team in 'A War Of Nerves' would have been something of a rarity.

Poorly equipped to begin with, the squads eventually had their own trucks or vans in which they carried sandbags, spades and picks, rope, winches, scaffolding and a few specialist items such as the tools required to open the casings and remove the fuses from bombs. As often as not, these tools had to be improvised, especially when the team came across a type of bomb or fuse on which they had never worked before. The three-man squads were organised as part of a unit that normally consisted of around 15 men, with each unit allocated one of 109 sections across the country as their 'patch'.

ABOVE: *When bomb disposal units were first formed in World War II they had little in the way of experience, training or equipment. Captain Hammond's team in 'War Of Nerves' were well-equipped with their own truck.*

The Blitz in 1940 left the bomb disposal teams with 2,000 unexploded bombs (or UXBs) to deal with before the end of August. By the time the war was over they were to have handled 45,441 bombs and 6,983 anti-aircraft shells. One of the problems they discovered with the German bombs was that many were designed not to go off on impact, but to penetrate deep inside a building before exploding. Even then, some were not designed to explode but to be left as dormant hazards that would detonate when later interfered with, either when the building was being cleared or when the bomb disposal teams tried to move them. Others were booby-trapped to go off specifically when an attempt was made to remove the fuse. During the war the heroes of the bomb disposal squads were awarded 13 George Crosses and 389 of them lost their lives.

Invasion

Set in April 1942, 'Invasion' tells the story of a group of Americans who arrive in Hastings to build an airfield from which an American bomber group will operate. Foyle is asked by the commanding officer of the American unit to give a talk to his men to try to make them feel welcome and a dance is organised, with the locals invited, to help foster good relations. In the meantime, Milner meets up with an old army friend, Will Grayson, who is home on leave. Will saved Milner's life in Trondheim and the two enjoy a drink together, although Will is anxious to find some whisky, a commodity that is becoming more and more scarce. Will is found dead in his locked bedroom after a fire breaks out at his house. Milner visits the scene and finds a whisky bottle that makes him believe there must be more to his friend's death than a simple accident. The night of the Americans' dance comes around and Sam attends, having been personally

ABOVE: *Captain John Kieffer (Jay Benedict), Sergeant Jack O'Connor (Corey Johnson), James Taylor (Peter Youngblood Hills) and Joe Farnetti (Jonah Lotan) were part of the unit of American engineers that made such a big impression when they began preparing an airfield for US bombers in 'Invasion'.*

ABOVE: *Milner, Sam and Foyle enjoy a brief off-duty moment at a dance hosted by the Americans.*

invited by a young American who has taken a shine to her. She has heard only recently in a letter from Andrew Foyle, with whom she has struck up a romance, that he has met someone else while posted far from home. At the dance, a local barmaid, who has been engaged to the son of the farmer whose land has been requisitioned to build the base but who has been dating one of the Americans, is found murdered. Foyle's investigation into her death reveals that she has been involved in producing illegal alcohol and helps Milner to understand why his friend Will has died in the fire.

When the American engineers arrive in 'Invasion' they are heard to discuss the problems of building the airfield they are there to construct, pumping water out of the site and making the ground ready to take the weight of a 'Fort'. The reference is to the 'Flying Fortress' or Boeing B-17 that formed the backbone of the United States Army Air Force bomber fleet in 1942. During the war there were around 700 air bases scattered all over Britain, just over 120 of them either specifically constructed for the USAAF, or converted for use by them. The majority of these bases were

on the flat land in East Anglia, Cambridgeshire and Lincolnshire, and the bombers that flew from Britain were designated the US Eighth Army Air Force under the command of Brigadier General Ira Eaker.

Following the attack on Pearl Harbor on 7 December 1941, US servicemen were embarking on ships bound for Britain before the New Year arrived and in early 1942 the first of the GIs (GI stood for General Issue) were enjoying British hospitality. This was the busiest time for airfield construction, with the building of two new bases beginning every week at an estimated cost of around £1 million each. British civilian contractors worked alongside the US engineers in shifting millions of tons of earth, removing many thousands of trees and installing an infrastructure for each base that was equivalent in terms of sewerage, water and electrical supply to that of a small town.

BELOW: *Ben Barrett (Tom Bennett) was understandably bitter when his girlfriend took up with James Taylor while he was away serving in the Royal Navy.*

ABOVE: *Joe Farnetti was totally smitten by Sam, whose relationship with Andrew Foyle had ended when he wrote to tell her he had met someone else.*

The first B-17s (although the USAAF flew other bombers as well) arrived in July 1942 and six weeks later they were in action on a raid against railway marshalling yards at Rouen in France. Ira Eaker joined one of the crews on that first mission. What Eaker really wanted, however, was for the Eighth to prove itself in attacks on Germany. His bomber groups used a tactic different to that of the RAF. They boasted a 'precision bombing' technique and proposed to fly missions in daylight, something the RAF had long since abandoned due to unacceptable losses. With the Flying Fortresses, however, Eaker believed that the tight formations could concentrate their firepower against enemy fighter planes. The first American sorties over Germany brought an acceptable loss rate, but by July 1943, 88 aircraft were lost in one week and when a force of 315 bombers were sent against the ball-bearing plant at Schweinfurt, deep inside Germany, 60 planes were shot down. Long range daylight missions were eventually cancelled until US fighter planes were developed that had a great enough range to escort the bombers all the way to their targets and back.

Meanwhile more and more US personnel were arriving in the UK. In the build-up to D-Day in June 1944 there were approximately 1.75 million GIs in Britain and during the course of the whole war around three million would pass through the country. They brought with them their culture, their music and their charm, and were frequently referred to as 'overpaid, oversexed and over here.'

An American soldier was very well-paid compared to his British counterpart, earning up to five times as much – and they were keen to spend it on enjoying themselves before having to face the rigours of battle. This regularly led to conflict with the locals, despite the fact that the US soldiers had been warned in a handbook entitled *Instructions for American Servicemen in Britain* not to appear brash by splashing money around and not to steal the British soldiers 'gals' while they were off fighting. The booklet attempted to explain the reserved attitude of the British, how they enjoyed playing sports even if they were no good at them and included tips such as 'The British don't know how to make a good cup of coffee. You don't know how to make a good cup of tea. It's an even swap' and 'stop and think before you sound off about lukewarm beer, or cold boiled potatoes and the way English cigarettes taste'.

The Americans took a great liking to British pubs, although British beer, which was vastly different to the lager-style beer they were used to back home, was difficult for them to get used to. Beer was not rationed, although supplies regularly ran low, but whisky became very difficult to find and many entrepreneurs turned to producing their own 'hooch' or 'moonshine' just like the alcohol on which Milner's friend became so drunk in 'Invasion'. On some bases, GIs with a pass that allowed them to go out on the town were given bottles of American whisky to make sure that they did not try to sample hooch. Some of the concoctions on offer were made with thinly disguised industrial alcohol. The air ministry issued a warning to RAF pilots about such illicit alcohol on sale in London clubs, stating that just a small amount might cause temporary blindness and getting drunk on the stuff could mean permanent blindness, insanity or death. They were not exaggerating. In May 1942 in Glasgow 14

ABOVE: *An American aircrew walk away from their B-17 'Flying Fortress', the type of aircraft destined for the airfield being prepared by Captain Kieffer's engineers. There were over 120 such bases in Britain during the war.*

people died after drinking hooch and four men in London were paralysed for 10 days after just one 'whisky' each in a hotel bar.

Bad Blood

Sam is in for a couple of surprises in 'Bad Blood'. Her young man from the American base asks her to marry him. It is clear that he is genuinely in love with her, but Sam needs time to consider whether this is the right time in her life to commit to marriage. Unfortunately, while she considers the proposal, she falls ill with a mysterious flu-like disease that leaves her body covered in black sores. Romance is also in the air for Milner, whose marriage has broken up, when he is visited by an old flame: Edith Ashford.

Edith's brother, Martin, a Conscientious Objector, is accused of murdering a naval hero after an argument in a pub. The sailor Tom Jenkins had been decorated for bravery after saving several shipmates from German aircraft and U-boats.

Although the murder happens outside Foyle's patch, he approaches the officer in charge of the area – an old army friend from the first war – and is allowed to look into the case. Martin Ashford had been working on a farm that, unlike the murder case, is on Foyle's patch and some sick cows have been stolen from the farmer. When Foyle pays him a visit, the farmer is more upset about his missing cattle than the murder and, after visiting the farm, Sam begins to feel ill.

BELOW: *Foyle falls foul of his old friend and colleague DCS Fielding when he interrupts the recovery of a body during a murder investigation.*

ABOVE: *Farmer Brian Jones (Kenneth Colley) calls in the vet Ted Cartwright (Roy Marsden) when his cows become afflicted with a mystery illness.*

When the wife of the murdered sailor dies of the same disease that has afflicted Sam, Foyle's investigation reveals the unsavoury truth about the murdered hero, brings him into contact with a military research group involved in secret experiments, and turns into a race against time to save Sam's life.

The experiments conducted by the scientists in 'Bad Blood' are based on the research carried out during the war at Porton Down in Wiltshire. It was there that Dr Paul Fildes was head of the N-bomb project, agent N being the codename given to anthrax. Anthrax is a bacterium carried in low levels by some animals, including sheep and cattle, but which can infect humans if it is swallowed, inhaled or passed through skin contact. In small doses skin contact may not prove fatal; the boils caused were at one time known as 'woolsorters' disease'. But inhalation of airborne anthrax spores proves fatal about 95 per cent of the time, even if the sufferer receives medical attention.

In July 1942, their tests at Porton Down having proved successful, Dr Fildes' team released their airborne version of anthrax on an island called Gruinard in Gruinard Bay off the west coast of Scotland between Ullapool and Gairloch. They needed to know whether anthrax could be used as a viable biological weapon in the open air and tested it against sheep, confined in crates just as was seen in

ABOVE: *Elsie Jenkins (Claire Cox) has to contend not only with the murder of her husband, but also a deadly disease when she is struck down by a strange virus.*

ABOVE: *Sheep were used in tests carried out with the Anthrax virus on Gruinard Island in Scotland, just as they were in 'Bad Blood'.*

'Bad Blood'. The sheep all developed flu-like symptoms, seemed to recover for a while, but then died within three or four days. Anthrax was never used as a weapon of war, the atomic bomb becoming the favoured weapon of mass destruction. It is believed, however, that as little as 100kg of the substance sprayed over a major population centre could kill up to three million people and make the city uninhabitable for decades. For years afterwards repercussions from the Gruinard tests were felt.

Local farmers on the mainland reported the mysterious deaths of sheep and cattle and, although it was not immediately admitted what kind of tests had taken place there, Gruinard Island was placed out of bounds. Anthrax proved so durable that the island remained in quarantine for 48 years despite attempts to eradicate the spores. In 1990 the island was finally judged to have been decontaminated, but some experts believe that buried anthrax spores can survive for hundreds of years and that even when some of the infected topsoil was removed from the island, the measures taken will not have been totally effective.

Like the anthrax experiments, the destruction of the convoy in 'Bad Blood' is based on fact. One of the greatest catastrophes of the war was suffered on the Atlantic convoy route when convoy PQ17 was attacked by wave after wave of bombers and a U-boat pack that stalked its ships relentlessly.

ABOVE: *Livestock on the fictional Brian Jones's farm were accidentally infected, reflecting the way that real farmers found their farm animals suffering during the Anthrax testing programme in Scotland.*

On 27 June 1942 the convoy left Iceland bound for the Soviet Union with a cargo or armaments destined for the Red Army, who were battling against the Germans on the Eastern Front. The Admiralty received information that a German naval battle group led by the battleship *Tirpitz* was preparing to attack the convoy and ordered the convoy to break formation and scatter.

The Tirpitz never materialised, but the Luftwaffe and the U-boat pack certainly did. July that far north in the Arctic Circle meant that there was almost 24 hours of daylight and the bombers could operate whenever the weather permitted. The U-boats simply had a field day. Over 100,000 tons of much-needed supplies were lost and 153 sailors died.

Allied warships were forbidden to help men struggling in the water and ordered to leave them to drown or freeze rather than have, for example, the 1,500 men on board a cruiser become sitting target for the U-boats. Had the convoy stayed together, the military escorts would have stood a better chance of fighting off the U-boats. As it was, only 11 of the 37 ships that left Iceland ever made it to the Soviet Union. The Navarino, as mentioned in 'Bad Blood,' was one of the ships lost.

Bleak Midwinter

Milner is put in an uncomfortable position when his wife, Jane, from whom he has allowed everyone to believe he is divorced, turns up in Hastings looking for reconciliation. He, of course, has become involved with Edith Ashford and wants nothing more to do with Jane. He finds himself in an even more difficult situation when Jane is murdered. It doesn't take Foyle long to work out that Jane's death is somehow connected to the death of Grace Philips, a munitions factory worker blown up while working on a production line.

The women who staffed the munitions factory in 'Bleak Midwinter' were working in an environment that many women who went into the factories during the war would instantly recognise. The labour crisis in 1941 led to the industrial conscription of women. Initially single women between the ages of 20 and 30 were obliged to register but the age range was later extended to 19 with an upper limit of 50 and married women were not exempt. By 1943 there were more than seven million in employment, a rise of more than two million from before the war. From a figure of seven per cent of the workforce in engineering, the female proportion grew to no less than 40 per cent, but this was not the first time women had flooded into the factories.

ABOVE: *Workers in munitions factories wore special overalls with no metal fastenings and could take no metal objects, not even a hair clip, onto the factory floor for fear of creating a spark.*

In World War I a shortage of manpower entailed the recruitment of an extra one million workers, but it was womanpower that solved the problem. Around 950,000 women went to work in munitions factories and a further 200,000 were employed in general engineering. They took up other jobs as well, of course, including working in garment factories producing khaki uniforms where the dye made their skin erupt in boils. But it was the 'munitionettes' producing explosives and gas components to fill shells that suffered the worst. Their greatest fear was the telltale yellowing of the eyes that meant they had been affected by the poison gas and were liable to fall ill. During World War II the safety precautions were far better. The World War I rules of

no metal hair-clips, jewellery or buttons with standard-issue overalls and rigorous inspections all to prevent a spark that could cause disaster still applied, but there were also special cosmetics and creams to protect the skin from exposure to chemicals. Yet still there were accidents. At the Aycliffe Royal Ordnance Factory in Newton Aycliffe near Darlington there were 17,000 workers, most of them women, who were known as the 'Aycliffe Angels'. There were several fatal accidents at the factory, four women dying in an explosion in 1942 and eight killed in a blast on 2 May 1945, less than a week before VE Day.

Despite the vital effort they put in and the fact that most women in industry were earning more than ever before, employers

ABOVE: *In 'Bleak Midwinter', Milner's personal life crossed over into his police work.*

ABOVE: *The munitions factory in 'Bleak Midwinter'.*

still tended to pay them less than male employees if they could get away with it. Neither were the unions much help in redressing the balance as they were run by men and, conscious that women made excellent welders and could operate lathes or tend machines every bit as well as most men, they were worried that there would be no jobs for the men when they returned from the war.

Casualties of War

Foyle has a bit of a shock when his god-daughter, Lydia, arrives on his doorstep. He hasn't seen anything of her for 10 years. With her is her young son, James, traumatised after his London school has been bombed and his classmates and teachers killed. Foyle lets them stay at his house, but then Lydia disappears. Sam is roped in as an unofficial nanny for the small boy as Foyle investigates illegal gambling and a series of sabotage incidents that lead to a murder at a secret research station where a new bomb is being developed. As the search for Lydia continues, Milner goes undercover to infiltrate the gambling network but is recognised as a policeman. He is saved from a beating after the game by two youths who intervene to fight off Milner's attackers. The young men have been losing heavily in the crooked game and Milner is to encounter them again when the sabotage investigation leads him and Foyle to a Spanish diplomat. Lydia is later discovered having attempted suicide, and Foyle invites her and James to come and live with him. The activities of the Spaniard and Foyle's frustration at the injustice of the situation he has uncovered during his investigation then lead him to consider his future as a police officer.

ABOVE: *Many women lost their lives in accidents in armaments factories, but the explosion that killed Grace Phillips (Sîan Brooke) was no accident.*

ABOVE: *In 1939 there were less than five million women in Britain in full time employment. By 1943 there were well over seven million, many employed in the highly dangerous munitions industry.*

ABOVE: *In 'Casualties of War', Foyle was forced to consider the contribution he was making as a police officer.*

The experiments with the spinning bomb, outlined in the 'Casualties Of War' episode, are based on the work of Sir Barnes Wallis and his team. Wallis was an engineer working in the aircraft industry, who had designed the R100 airship as well as the Vickers Wellesley and Wellington bombers. The spinning bomb was intended to skip across the surface of the reservoirs behind the Möhne, Eder and Sorpe dams in Germany, avoiding the torpedo nets that protected the structures, before hitting the dams and sinking below the surface where it would finally explode. Wallis experimented with spinning marbles in an old tin bath in his garden in Effingham in Surrey before two different versions of

the bomb were built, one spherical and one shaped like an oil barrel. Tests like the one depicted in 'Casualties Of War' were carried out on The Fleet, the lagoon behind Chesil Beach near Weymouth, and off Reculver near Herne Bay on the north Kent coast, as well as at Loch Striven in Scotland. The Nant-y-Gor dam in the Elan Valley in Wales was also destroyed during tests before the mission was launched against Germany's Ruhr Valley in May 1943. Of the 19 Lancaster bombers from 617 Squadron (afterwards known as The Dambusters), eight were lost during the mission, with 53 of the 56 airmen killed. Both the Möhne and Eder dams were breached, however, causing damage and

ABOVE: *Foyle was in for a shock when his God-daughter, Lydia showed up on his doorstep along with her son, James (Joshua Lewis).*

ABOVE: *Frank (Gerard Kearns) and Terry Morgan (Harry Eden) saved Milner from a beating but were later forced to commit acts of sabotage by a high-ranking foreign diplomat.*

flooding to power stations, factories and coal mines up to 100 miles from the dams. It took many months for the industrial areas to recover and for the Germans to rebuild the dams.

Milner's infiltration of an illegal gambling den in 'Casualties Of War' reflects a widespread gambling problem during the war years. Organisers of gambling clubs were not deterred by fines of up to £350 when there was so much easy money to be made, not only in underground clubs in London but also in factories and shipyards all over the country. Police knew that when they raided clubs in London they stood to collar not only professional criminals running the gaming rackets but also a motley collection of deserters and draft dodgers. It was more difficult for a police raid to contain the suspects at ad-hoc gambling venues like the one in which Milner manages to become involved. 'Crown and anchor', the game being played in 'Casualties Of War', was a game where dice marked with crowns and anchors were cast on a crown and anchor board or cloth. It was a favourite game at Southampton docks where up to 300 men would gather to participate. Members of the Army Intelligence Corps worked with the CID to infiltrate the group, the undercover Intelligence men each grabbing hold of one of the organisers to prevent him melting into the escaping crowd when the police raid began.

Incidents of sabotage like those committed by the two youths in 'Casualties Of War' were not unknown during the war and foreign embassies were certainly involved in running, or attempting to run, spy rings. The Spanish, although ostensibly neutral, were sympathetic to the Germans and Fascist rabble-rousers in Spain even organised crowds to stone the

British Embassy in Madrid. Both Spain and Portugal were hotbeds of espionage where both sides attempted to recruit seamen or travellers to do their bidding. Spaniard Juan Pujol became a German agent in 1941, offering his services to German Intelligence agents in Madrid. He then began a truly remarkable double life, betraying the Germans – whom he hated – and contacting MI6 in Spain, who arranged for his transfer to London. There he was passed to MI5, working under the codename 'Garbo' with a Spanish-speaking officer to create a huge network of 27 agents scattered throughout the UK – all imaginary. Throughout the war they fed false information to the Germans, including misinformation about D-Day, so successfully that they are today believed to have been responsible for the Germans' apparent lack of interest in attempting to infiltrate other high-quality agents into the country.

Nevertheless, there were others willing to pass information to the Germans via foreign embassies. In 1940, Russian émigrée Anna Wolkoff conspired with US Embassy cipher clerk Tyler Kent, both members of the pro-Fascist Right Club, to pass details of messages Kent smuggled out of the US Embassy, including correspondence between Churchill and Roosevelt, to the enemy via both the Italian and Romanian Embassies. Sadly for them, MI5 had infiltrated the Right Club before the war and they were arrested. Kent was sentenced to seven years in prison but was deported to the United States in 1945, and Wolkoff was given ten years.

Acknowledgements

This book would not have been possible without the help and advice of many people. I would like to thank Anthony Horowitz for talking to me about the characters he so skilfully creates and Terry Charman of the Imperial War Museum for taking the time to discuss *Foyle's War* and the way people lived in the 1940s. The book certainly could not have happened without Jill Green, head of Greenlit Rights, and Catherine Oldfield of Greenlit, who did a sterling job keeping me supplied with scripts and plot synopses. The staff at Hastings Library were most helpful, not least in providing wartime copies of the *Hastings and St Leonard's Observer* for me to browse through. For her encouragement and patience, thanks must certainly also go to my editor at Carlton Books, Lorna Russell.

Bibliography/webography

A number of books and websites proved invaluable in researching this book and deserve a special mention.

Angus Calder's excellent book *The People's War* (Jonathan Cape, 1969) is a mine of information about WWII as is the hugely entertaining *An Underground At War* by Donald Thomas (John Murray, 2003). *WWII: The People's Story* by Nigel Fountain (Reaer's Digest, 2003) uses material from the Imperial War Museum's sound archive and is a wonderful insight into the experiences of ordinary people during the war as is *Women At War* (Nigel Fountain, Michael O'Mara Books, 2002) which draws on the same source. Norman Longmate's *If Britain Had Fallen* (BBC with Hutchinson & Co., 1972) is a chilling look at what might have happened had the Germans crossed the channel. *Hastings At War* 1939-45 by Nathan Dylan Goodwin (Phillimore & Co., 2005) is packed with information, interviews and photographs and the promotional booklet produced by Hastings Borough Council, *Foyle's Hastings*, includes some wonderful photographs and snippets about the making of the show. *Mad Frank's Diary* by Frankie Fraser with James Morton (Virgin Publishing, 2000) has some good gangland memories of WWII and at the other end of the scale, *Some Were Spies* by The Earl Jowitt (Hodder & Stoughton, 1954) is a fascinating memoir from the former Solicitor General. Finally, *The Encyclopedia of Executions* is an exhaustive work by John J. Eddleston with details of every execution carried out in Britain in the 20th century.

Websites from which information was gleaned include:
www.bawdseyradargroup.co.uk
www.kent-police-museum.co.uk
www.mi5.gov.uk
www.mi6.gov.uk
www.answers.com
http://en.wikipedia.org
www.queenvic.demon.co.uk
www.blondmcindoe.com
www.historylearningsite.co.uk
http://news.bbc.co.uk
www.communist-party.org.uk
www.dambusters.org.uk
www.computing.dundee.ac.uk
www.spartacus.schoolnet.co.uk
www.learningcurve.gov.uk
www.unionhistory.info
www.aycliffeangels.org.uk
www.norfolkbroads.com
www.foyleswar.com
www.schools.bedfordshire.gov.uk
www.italian-heritage-ancoats.org.uk
www.gcal.ac.uk